REASONS FOR READING

STUDENTS' BOOK
Evelyn Davies and Norman Whitney

WESTMINSTER COLLEGE
CASTLE LANE
VICTORIA
LONDON, SW1 6DR
ENGLAND

HEINEMANN EDUCATIONAL BOOKS
LONDON

Heinemann Educational Books Ltd.
22 Bedford Square, London WC1B 3HH

LONDON   EDINBURGH   MELBOURNE   AUCKLAND
HONG KONG   SINGAPORE   KUALA LUMPUR   NEW DELHI
IBADAN   NAIROBI   JOHANNESBURG
EXETER (NH)   KINGSTON   PORT OF SPAIN

> *Reasons for Reading* is published together with an accompanying *Teachers' Guide* (ISBN   O 435 28037 6)

ISBN 0 435 280368

© Evelyn Davies and Norman Whitney   1979
First published 1979

Design and artwork by Hedgehog Design

Set in Univers and Plantin
Printed and bound in Great Britain by
Spottiswoode Ballantyne Ltd., London and Colchester

CONTENTS

To the Teacher
To the Student   iv

Section 1
Reading for Information

Focus on . . . topic.

Unit
1 People   2
2 Places   6
3 Directions   10
4 Journeys   14
5 Notices   18
Reading Revision 1   22

Section 2
Reading for Meaning

Focus on . . . function.

1 Instructions   26
2 Messages   30
3 Facts   34
4 Opinions   38
5 Persuasion   42
Reading Revision 2   46

Section 3
Reading for Pleasure

Focus on . . . text.

1 Picture Stories   50
2 Magazines   54
3 Non-fiction   58
4 Fiction   62
5 A Theatre Visit   66
Reading Revision 3   70

Index of different Text Types   75

To the Teacher

REASONS FOR READING is the first book in a new course in Reading Comprehension.

AIMS

The aims of the course are:

- to help students recognize, read, understand and enjoy a wide variety of text types in English.
- to help students to apply to English the skills they already have in their first language.
- to support those modern EFL course books which need good reading skills for their proper use and understanding.

LEVEL

This first book is intended for elementary to mid-intermediate students of English as a Foreign Language, and is designed to fit into the second or third year of many secondary and adult courses.

For teachers who know the *Heinemann Guided Readers* the language level corresponds with the Elementary and Intermediate levels of the series.

SPECIAL FEATURES

Reasons for Reading has a *STORYLINE*—one day in the life of two students in London.
Their needs for reading in English provide the functional context for a variety of authentic text types.

At the end of each unit of work there is a *SKILLS CHECK*. This summarizes for the student the kind of text read and the particular reading skills used.

There are a wide variety of *STUDENT ACTIVITIES* in the book, including writing and speaking practice.

The normal pattern of text followed by questions has been rejected in favour of integrated skills work appropriate to each particular text type.

There is an accompanying *TEACHERS' GUIDE*. This gives help in how to use the book, and ideas for further practice with the exercise types introduced in the book, which include information questions, multiple-choice items, true/false practice, cloze work and study skills activities.

To the Student

REASONS FOR READING will help you to prepare yourself for reading English easily and confidently.

Much of the work in this book is to help you to read texts which at first may look 'difficult' or strange. If you are already a good reader, you know that you do not always have to understand every word of a text. This book will help you to apply this skill to English texts.

There are *THREE SECTIONS* in the book:

1 INFORMATION

This section will help you to recognize and use the kind of text which gives factual information—such as forms, maps, charts, plans and notices.

2 MEANING

This section helps you to recognize and understand the function and purpose of texts, and how these relate to the kind of language the writer uses.

3 PLEASURE

This section helps you to read a variety of real texts, fiction and non-fiction from different sources such as books, magazines, comics, brochures and programmes.

Each Section has *FIVE UNITS* of four pages each.

The first two pages are about the characters in the book, and *their* reasons for reading.

The second two pages develop the reading skills they need and apply these skills to other similar situations or texts.

Each Section is followed by *READING REVISION*.

SECTION 1
Reading for Information

Reading for Information 1. PEOPLE

Read this DESCRIPTION. ▼

Rosa Morello is from Colombia in South America. She is a student. She has come to London to study English.

Rosa is eighteen years old and single. She has dark hair, dark brown eyes and is 1.65m tall. She likes pop music, dancing, reading and good food. She is also interested in travel and languages.

In London, Rosa lives in a small flat with her friend Linda Morris. The flat is in north London.

Read this FORM. ▼

Dolores of London   High Fashion
Piccadilly, London W.1.

CONFIDENTIAL   STAFF RECORD CARD

- SURNAME: MORRIS
- FIRST NAME: Linda
- SEX: Female
- MARITAL STATUS: Single
- ADDRESS: 144A Canfield Gardens, London NW6
- TELEPHONE: 01-794-6009
- DATE OF BIRTH: 18-6-58
- NATIONALITY: British
- HEIGHT: 5' 8"
- PRESENT POST: Sales assistant, Shoe Department
- INTERESTS: Music, dancing, theatre
- AMBITION: Wants to manage the Dress Department
- SIGNED: M. Lewis
- DATE: Jan 10 1979

Michael Lewis. Personnel Officer.   Ref. LM/ML/F/79

READING FOR INFORMATION 1 PEOPLE

Read this LETTER. ▼

Stockholm
Sweden
April 20

The Director,
Pembroke College,
Pembroke Road,
London, W.8.

Dear Sir/Madam
    I am coming to London in the summer to improve my English. Please send me an application form for your English classes. A friend of mine (also Swedish) studied at Pembroke College last year. He enjoyed it very much.
    I am twenty-two years old. I have studied English for eight years. I know English Grammar quite well.
    Do you have any special courses in technical English? I am an engineering student, and I would like to improve my knowledge of technical language.
    Please send me details about accommodation and about fees.
               yours faithfully,
                Carl Lindström

1

① Find information about:

Rosa

Which country does she come from?

How old is she?

Why has she come to London?

What sort of music does she like?

Linda

Where does she work?

When was she born?

How tall is she?

What is her job?

Carl

What is his surname?

What is his nationality?

When is he coming to London?

What sort of English does he want to learn?

② Complete this form for Rosa.

INTERNATIONAL STUDENT TRAVEL	
SURNAME ...MORELLO...............	FIRST NAMES ....
SEX	NATIONALITY ....
ADDRESS	TELEPHONE ....
....	
AGE	Attach passport photograph here:
HEIGHT	
COLOUR OF HAIR	
COLOUR OF EYES	
OCCUPATION	
INTERESTS	
....	

③ Write a description of Linda.
Use about 60 words. You can begin:

Linda Morris is from London in England. She is ....

....

READING FOR INFORMATION 1 PEOPLE

2

① Draw a form like Rosa's, and complete it with information about yourself. Exchange forms with a friend, and write a description of your friend, in English. Then read the description to your friend. What does he/she think of it?

② Now make and fill in a CHART for your class.
Like this: ▶

```
INTERNATIONAL STUDENT TRAVEL
SURNAME ..........         FIRST NAMES ..........
SEX ..........             NATIONALITY ..........
ADDRESS ..........         TELEPHONE ..........
                           Attach passport photograph here:
AGE ..........
HEIGHT ..........
COLOUR OF HAIR ..........
COLOUR OF EYES ..........
OCCUPATION ..........
INTERESTS ..........
```

PERSONAL INFORMATION CHART

Surname	First Name	Sex	Age	Height (metric)	Height (English)	Date of Birth
SCHORN	Heinz	Male	14	1.58	5' 3"	8-9-64
BAUM	Sabine					

3

① Use the TABLE to find your height.

Example:

Rosa is 1.65m tall.

In the metric system
100cm = 1m
One hundred centimetres
equals one metre.

Linda is 5' 8" tall.

In the English-speaking world
12" = 1'
Twelve inches equals one foot.

Rosa is 1.65m or 5' 6" tall.
Linda is 5' 8" or 1.70m tall.

A TABLE

" inches	' feet	cm	m
1		2.5	
6		15	
8		20	
10		25	
12	1	30	
24	2	60	
36	3	90	
48	4	120	1.2
60	5	150	1.5
72	6	180	1.8

Note: 1 cm = approx. ½"
One centimetre equals approximately half an inch.

READING FOR INFORMATION **1 PEOPLE**

② Use the chart and a tape measure to find your English measurements.

Men's clothes

Collar		Waist		Chest	
cm	ins	cm	ins	cm	ins
36	14	71	28	81	32
38	15	76	30	84	33
39/40	15½	81	32	86	34

Women's clothes

Size	Bust/hip	Bust/hip	Waist	
	ins	cm	ins	cm
8	30/32	76/81	23	58
10	32/34	81/86	24	61
12	34/36	86/91	26	66
14	36/38	91/97	28	71
16	38/40	97/102	30	76

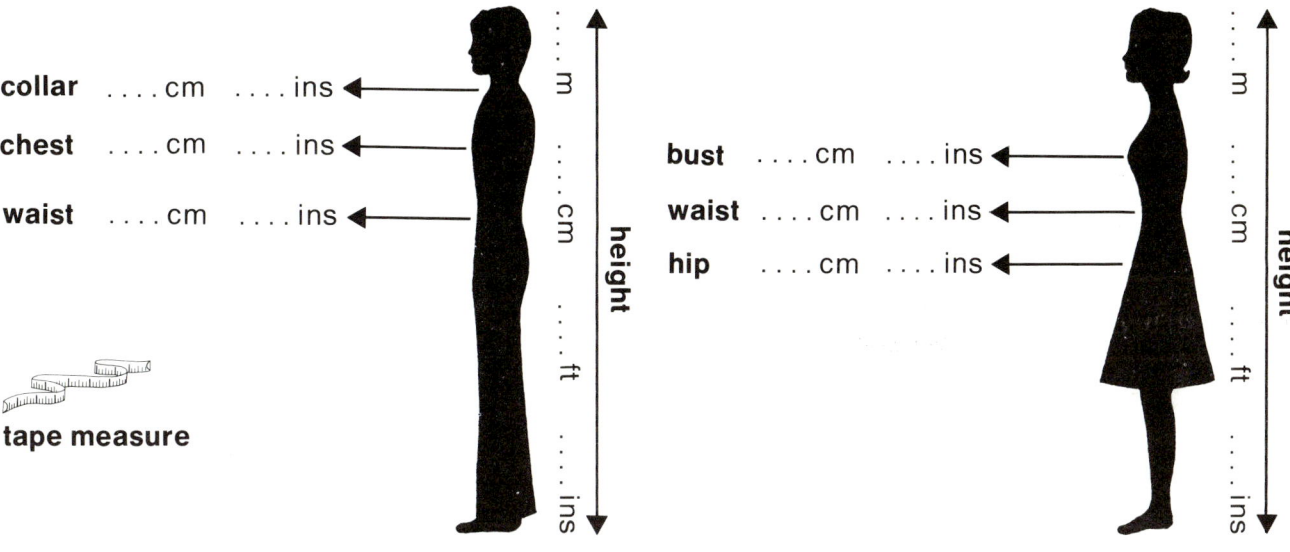

collar ....cm ....ins
chest ....cm ....ins
waist ....cm ....ins

tape measure

bust ....cm ....ins
waist ....cm ....ins
hip ....cm ....ins

skills check

You have read:
A description......of Rosa.
A form......about Linda.
A letter......from Carl.

You have practised: **1 Reading abbreviations.**

Examples:
1.65m — one metre (and) sixty-five centimetres
5′ 8″ — five feet eight inches
18-6-58 — the eighteenth of June (*or* June the eighteenth) nineteen fifty-eight
Jan. — January
London W1 — London west one
London NW6 — London north west six

2 Reading charts and tables.

Examples:

cm	ins	cm	ins	cm	ins
36	14	71	28	81	32
38	15	76	30	84	33
39/40	15½	81	32	86	34

Eighty-four centimetres equals thirty-three inches.
Thirty-two inches equals eighty-one centimetres.

READING FOR INFORMATION 2 PLACES

Reading for Information
2. PLACES

It's Rosa's first day at college, and she asks Linda how to get there.

Rosa This is the address. How do I find it?

Linda You need a London street map. Here it is!

A STREET MAP

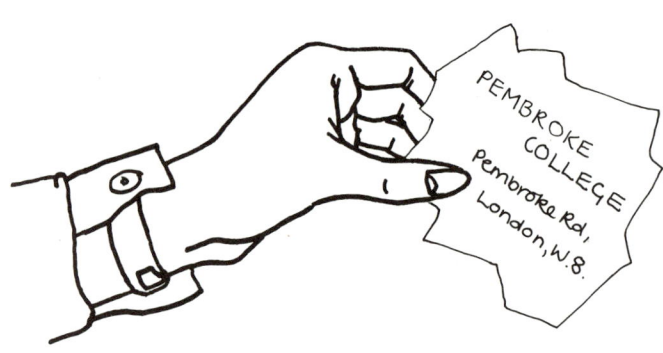

An INDEX ▼

```
Pembroke Av. Surb – 3D 103     Pennine La. NW2 – 4D 27
Pembroke Clo. SW1 – 2F 62b     Pennington St. E1 – 4D 61d
Pembroke Clo. Mitc – 2C 106    Penn La. Bex – 1D 101
Pembroke Gdns. W8 – 4E 59      Penn Rd. N7 – 1F 45
Pembroke Gdns Clo. W8 –        Penn St. N1 – 3C 46
  4E 59                        Pennyfields. E14 – 2C 64
Pembroke M. W8 – 4E 59         Pennymoor Wlk. W9 – 4E 43
Pembroke Pl. W8 – 3E 59        Penpoll Rd. E8 – 2F 47
Pembroke Pl. Edgw – 3A 12      Penpool La. Well – 4C 84
Pembroke Pl. Iswth – 2D 71     Penrhyn Av. E17 – 4F 19
Pembroke Rd. E17 – 2C 32       Penrhyn Cres. E17 – 4F 19
Pembroke Rd. N8 – 1F 29        Penrhyn Cres. SW14 – 3E 73
Pembroke Rd. N10 – 3A 16       Penrhyn Gro. E17 – 4F 19
Pembroke Rd. N13 – 1F 17       Penrhyn Rd. King – 3B 102
Pembroke Rd. N15 – 2D 31       Penrith Pl. SE27 – 2A 94
Pembroke Rd. SE25 – 3C 108     Penrith Rd. N15 – 2C 30
Pembroke Rd. W8 – 4E 59        Penrith Rd. N Mald – 3F 103
Pembroke Rd. Brom – 2B 112     Penrith Rd. T Hth – 2B 108
Pembroke Rd. Gnfd – 4C 38      Penrith St. SW16 – 4D 93
```

Rosa Where's Pembroke Road?

Linda The index says Pembroke Road west eight, is in square four E on page fifty-nine.

A GRID MAP ▼

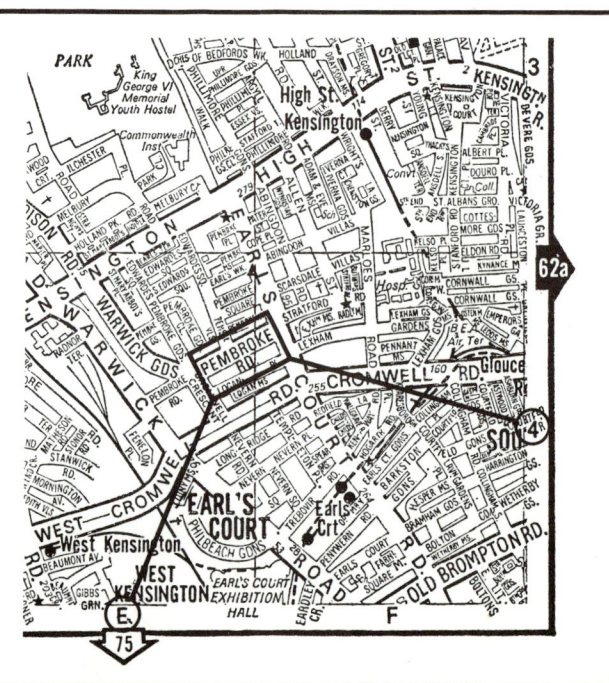

Rosa I've found page fifty-nine, but where is Pembroke Road? Where is it on the map?

Linda It's a grid map. Look. Four . . . E . . . Pembroke Road. Good! We've found it.

READING FOR INFORMATION **2 PLACES**

Rosa But how do I get *there* from *here*? Where is it in *London*?

Linda Let me show you. We live here, in square number forty-three. Your college is in Kensington, in square fifty-eight or fifty-nine.

An AREA MAP and a SCALE ▼

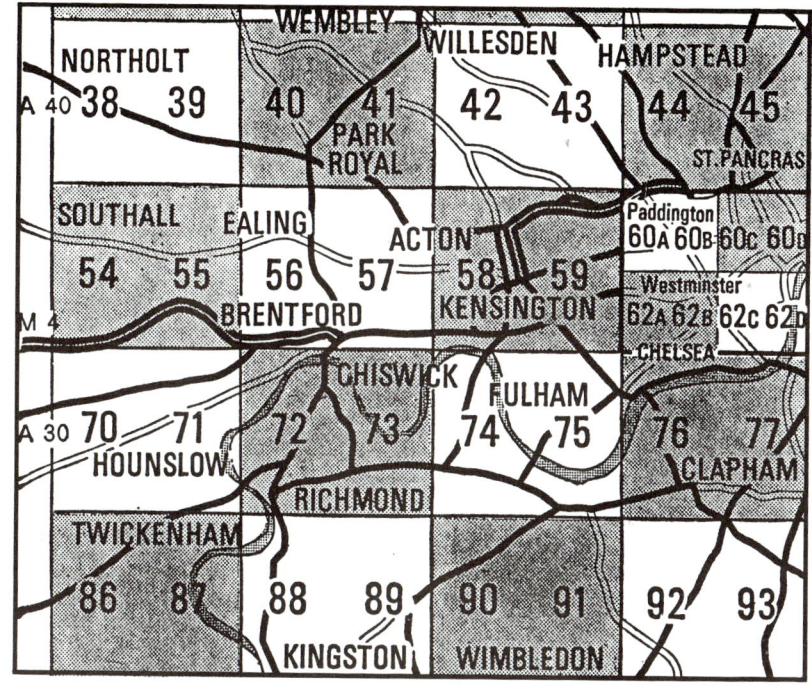

1

① Rosa is going to Kensington. Look at the area map. Kensington is in square 58 and 59: fifty-eight and fifty-nine.

1 Change these numbers into words:

   9   28   146   3,864   57,276

2 Change these words into numbers:

seven   sixty-one   three hundred and forty-two

five thousand nine hundred and fifteen

eighty-eight thousand one hundred and one

3 In square number forty-four, you can find Hampstead.

What can you find in:

57   41   42   75   76?

4 You can find Brentford in square number fifty-six. Where can you find:

St Pancras   Ealing   Wimbledon Paddington   Chelsea?

5 Linda and Rosa live in Hampstead. Rosa's college is in Kensington.

How far is it from Hampstead to Kensington?

From Richmond to Chelsea?

From Kensington to Wimbledon?

② Use the index and key below to tell a friend how to find an address in London. Like this:

A Where's South Hill Park Gardens, north-west three?

B It's on page forty-four, in square one B.

or

A Where's Southland Road, south-east eighteen?

B It's on page eighty-four, in square two B.

INDEX

Southey St. SE20 – 1F 109
Southfield Cotts. W3 – 3E 55
Southfield Pk. Harrow – 1C 22
Southfield Rd. N17 – 4A 18
Southfield Rd. W4 – 3E 57
Southfields NW4 – 4E 13
Southfields Rd. SW18 – 1E 91
Southgate Gro. N1 – 3C 46

South Gro. N6 – 3D 29
South Gro. E19 – 2B 32
South Hill Av. W6 – 4D 23
South Hill Pk. NW3 – 1B 44
S. Hill Pk. Gdns. NW3 – 1B 44
S. Island Pl. SW9 – 2A 78
Southland Rd. SE18 – 2B 84

KEY

Av: Avenue	**Pk:** Park
Cotts: Cottages	**Pl:** Place
E: East	**Rd:** Road
Gdns: Gardens	**St:** Street
Gro: Grove	**SE:** South-East
N: North	**SW:** South-West
NW: North-West	**W:** West

7

READING FOR INFORMATION **2 PLACES**

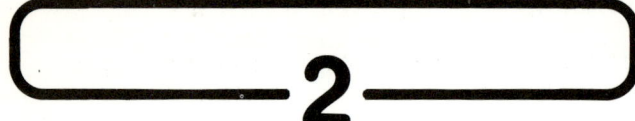

① On this grid map of Spain, Madrid is in square **Db**. Find the squares for:

Valencia Malaga Santander Zaragoza Barcelona

In square **Da** you can find Bilbao. Find the places in the following squares:

Dd Cc Cb Fb Ed

② Look at the list of countries below. Put them into alphabetical order.
Begin: Australia,

Then, match each country with its international car registration, to make an index.

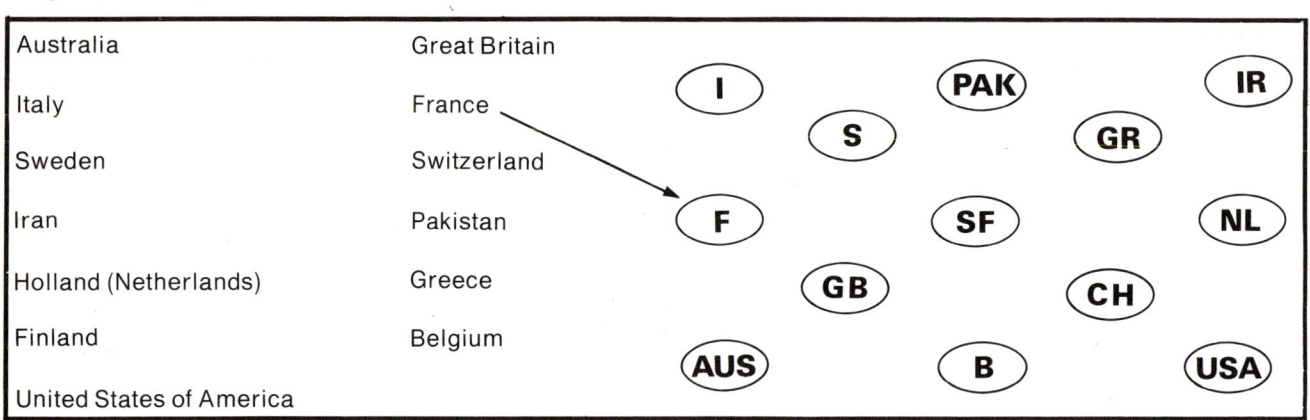

③ Read this address:

```
24A, Lincoln Street,
South York Avenue,
Boston,
United States of America

Twenty-Second of February 1979
Sunday.
```

Here is the same address with eight abbreviations. Can you find them?

24A, Lincoln St,
S. York Ave,
Boston,
U.S.A.
22nd Feb. '79
Sun.

Thank you for your last letter.
Been very busy shopping and

Rewrite this address **using abbreviations**:

```
144A, Canfield Gardens,
      Hampstead,
      London north-west six
      Great Britain

Monday the thirty-first of December
```

Write this address out **in full**:

```
44, Palewell Pk.,
   E. Sheen,
      London SW14
Wed. 17th Oct.
```

READING FOR INFORMATION **2 PLACES**

3

① Look quite quickly at this text from an English newspaper, and find a MAP, an INDEX and a KEY.

WEATHERWISE

HIGH pressure ridge will decline, and troughs of low pressure will cross Britain from the north-west later. Until mid-week England – except some northern areas – and Wales will be mostly dry apart from some drizzle in the west and the threat of thundery showers over southern England today. Sunny periods are likely in most parts with near-average temperatures generally. Unsettled weather is likely to extend to most areas in the second part of the week. Rain is expected, particularly in northern and western regions but sunny dry periods are also likely, chiefly in many central and southern areas. Temperatures will range from rather below average in the north to rather above in the south.

The forecast for today
SUNNY spells. Outlook: unchanged.

District Forecasts Key
1, 2, 3, 5, 6, 7, 15: Dry. Sunny
4, 8, 9, 10: Cloudy
11, 12, 13, 16, 17, 18, 21: Dry. Sunny.

14, 19, 20, 22, 23, 29: Mainly dry.
24, 25, 26, 27, 28: Rather cloudy. Occasional light rain.

Warmest: Jersey and Southampton 23c 73f. **Coolest:** Lerwick (Shetlands) 6c 43f. **Wettest:** Tiree (Hebrides) 0.01 in. **Sunniest:** Torquay 14.2 hr. **London:** Max 21c 70f. Min. 13c 55f. Sun. 6.5 hr. Rain: nil. Barometer (7 p.m.): 1021.4 mb, 30.16 in., falling. Humidity: 53 per cent.

INDEX
Birmingham	7
Belfast	29
Brighton	2
Bristol	9
Cardiff	10
Dover	2
Derby	15
Edinburgh	17
Leeds	16
London	1
Manchester	12
Oxford	3

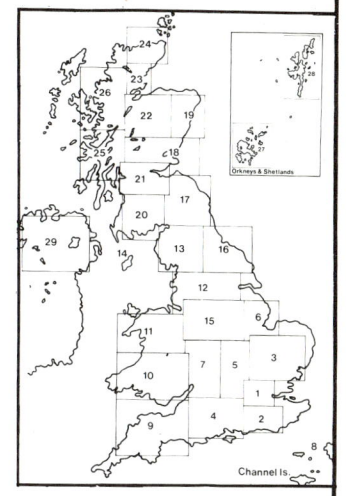

World Weather

KEY   C = Cloudy   R = Raining   S = Sunny

Amsterdam	C 16°	Bermuda	R 29°	Cologne	C 18°	Geneva	S 23°	L. Palmas	S 24°	Moscow	C 22°	Paris	S 21°	Tunis	S 31°
Barcelona	S 27°	Biarritz	S 23°	Copenhagen	C 14°	Guernsey	S 19°	Madrid	S 37°	Munich	S 19°	Rome	S 28°	Vancouver	C 16°
Belgrade	S 23°	Bristol	S 17°	Dubrovnik	S 28°	Helsinki	R 15°	Majorca	S 26°	New York	C 22°	Tel Aviv	S 29°	Venice	S 26°
		Budapest	R 20°	Florence	S 30°	Jersey	S 21°	Malaga	S 24°	Nice	S 25°	Tenerife	S 24°	Vienna	R 21°

② Now, look at the text again. Then, with a friend, ask and answer questions about the weather. Like this:

Great Britain

(check map index)
- A Where's London?
- B It's in square one.

(check District Forecasts key)
- A What's the weather like?
- B It's dry and sunny.

The World

(Check World index)
- A What's the temperature in Amsterdam?
- B It's sixteen degrees.

(check key)
- A What's the weather like?
- B It's cloudy.

skills check

You have read:
- **A street map** ...... of a city.
- **An index** ...... of cities.
- **A grid map** ...... of a country.
- **A weather forecast** ...... from a newspaper.

You have practised: **1 Reading more abbreviations.**

Examples:
St.	Street	GB	Great Britain
N.	North	Wed.	Wednesday
21st.	twenty-first	°	degrees

2 Using a key or an index to read maps and charts.

Example: London 1
1 ...... Dry and Sunny   'It's dry and sunny in London.'

READING FOR INFORMATION 3 DIRECTIONS

Reading for Information
3. DIRECTIONS

Rosa is ready to leave the flat, and asks Linda for DIRECTIONS.

Linda   Hurry! You'll be late!

Rosa   But I don't know where to go!

Linda   Don't worry. First you go to the station.

Rosa   How do I get there?

Linda   Don't worry. It's easy. Turn right. Cross to the other side of the road. Stay on the left. Go straight along this road. When you get to the main road, the station is on the left. Good luck! Don't get lost!

But Rosa *did* get lost. A few minutes later she stopped, and thought...

Rosa   Oh dear, I'm lost. Did Linda say '*stay* on the left' or 'turn left'? I can't remember.

Rosa   Excuse me. Can you help me? I'm looking for the station.

Man   It isn't far from here. Go straight along this road for about two hundred yards. Turn left...

Rosa   Wait please! Two hundred yards, straight along.

Man   Yes. Then turn left.

Rosa   Left.

Man   Yes. Walk straight along for about twenty yards...

Rosa   Straight for twenty yards.

Man   And the station is on the left.

Rosa   Thanks. I hope I get there this time!

READING FOR INFORMATION **3 DIRECTIONS**

① This map shows three places:

Linda's flat	**A**
The station	**B**
Where Rosa got lost	**C**

1 With a pencil, follow Linda's directions.

'When you get out of the house, turn right. Cross the road. Stay on the left. Go straight along. When you get to the main road, the station is on your left.'

2 Now, with the pencil, follow Rosa's mistakes.

She went out of the house, and turned right. She crossed the road. She went straight along, and took the first turning on the left. She went straight along again, and took the second turning on the right.

3 What is the name of the main road where the station is?

4 Which road did Rosa think was the main road?

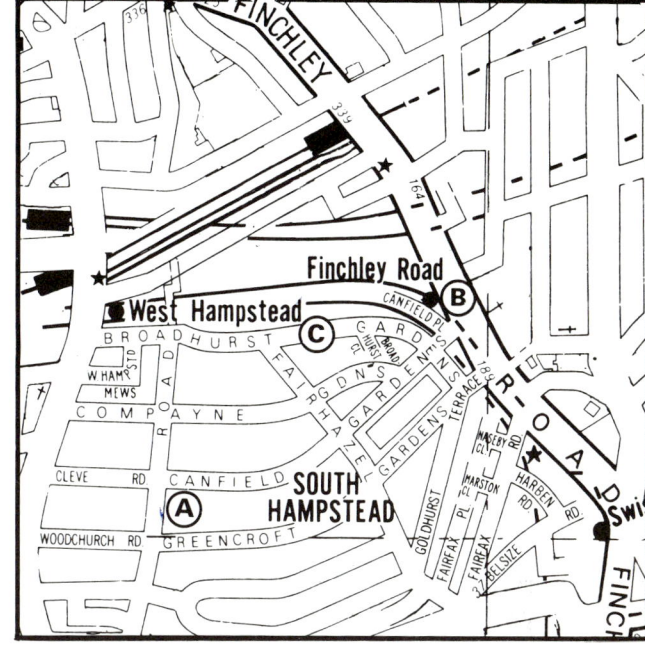

②  means 'turn left'.

Can you match these signs and DIAGRAMS with their written directions?

    Turn left.   Take the third turning on the right.

 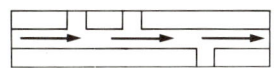   Don't turn right. Go straight along.

 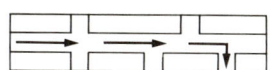 Turn right.   Don't turn left.

③ Read Linda's directions again. Can you draw a diagram to help Rosa?

④ Draw a map from your home to the nearest station, bus stop or airport. Then write some directions in English to match it.

READING FOR INFORMATION 3 DIRECTIONS

2

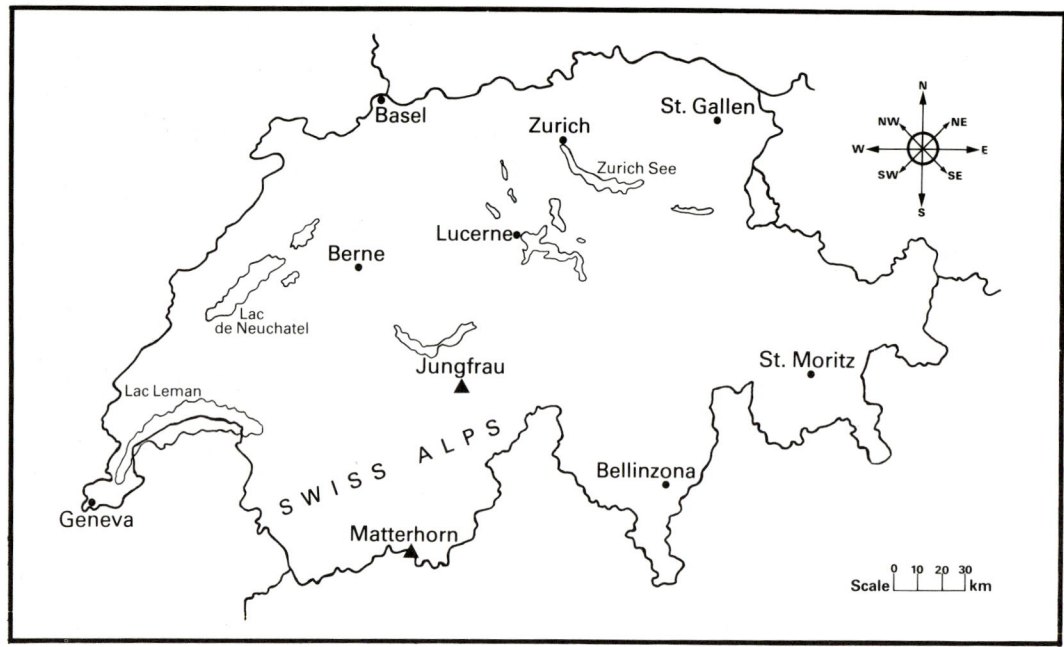

① Berne is in the north-west of Switzerland.

Where are: **St Moritz   Basel   Bellinzona   St Gallen   Geneva?**

St Gallen is 60 km east of Zurich.

Where are: **Lucerne from Zurich   Berne from Bellinzona   Zurich from Berne?**

② Use the chart below to tell a friend, as quickly as you can, where places are.

Ask and answer questions, like this:

> A   Where's Oxford?
> B   Oxford is a hundred kilometres west of London.

DESTINATION	DIRECTION	DISTANCE	START
Birmingham	S	110km	Manchester
Bruges	W	80km	Antwerp
Madrid	SW	500km	Andorra
Nancy	E	300km	Paris
Naples	SE	250km	Rome
Naxos	SE	180km	Athens
Oslo	NW	550km	Stockholm
Oxford	W	100km	London
Perugia	N	120km	Rome
St Gallen	E	60km	Zurich

READING FOR INFORMATION **3 DIRECTIONS**

3

This is a plan of the British Museum, ▶
and this is a message about a meeting there. ▼

Dear Marge,
Meet me in the Coffee Shop at the British Museum. Go in the Main Entrance. Turn right into Room 29. Go straight through and carry on into Room 30. The Coffee Shop is straight ahead. See you at 11 am.
Don't be late.
Love D.

① Follow the directions in the message, by reading the plan.

② Use the plan and the key to give written or spoken directions for these places:

1 From the Main Entrance to room thirty-two.

2 From the Bookshop to the Disabled Lavatories.

3 From the North Entrance to the Art of Islam.

4 From the Coffee Shop to the Map Gallery.

5 From room eight to room twenty-five. What will you see there?

You can use phrases like:

Turn	left right	Go straight	ahead along through on
Carry on	into . . . as far as . . .		

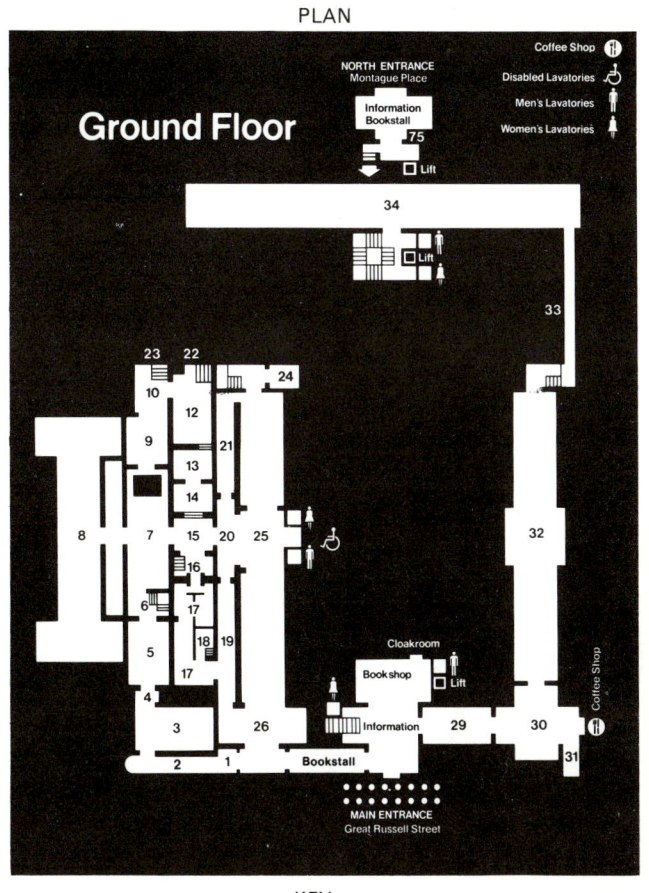

PLAN

Ground Floor

(Plan of the British Museum Ground Floor, showing North Entrance (Montague Place), Information Bookstall, Lifts, numbered rooms, Cloakroom, Bookshop, Information Bookstall, Coffee Shop, and Main Entrance (Great Russell Street). Icons indicate Coffee Shop, Disabled Lavatories, Men's Lavatories, Women's Lavatories.)

KEY

British Library Galleries
29 Illuminated manuscripts
30 Historical, musical and literary manuscripts
31 Bible Room
32 King's Library
33 Map Gallery

Egyptian
25 Egyptian Sculpture

Greek and Roman
1/2 Greek Bronze Age
3 Archaic Greece
4 Room of the Kouroi
5 Room of the Harpy Tomb
6 Bassae Room
7 Nereid Room
8 Sculptures from the Parthenon (Elgin Marbles)
9 Caryatid Room
10 Payava Room
12 Mausoleum Room
13 Hellenistic Art
14/15 Roman Art

Oriental
34 Art of Islam, South and South East Asia, China and Korea

Western Asiatic
17 Assyrian Saloon
19/20 Nimrud
21 Nineveh
24 Ancient Palestine

skills check

You have read: **Written directions**

Spoken directions

A map and a scale

A plan and key

You have practised: **1 Reading directions**

Examples: 'the station is on the left.'
Go in the main entrance.

2 Reading abbreviations for direction and distance.

Example: 250km SE
'two hundred and fifty kilometres south-east.'

3 Using plans and diagrams to give directions in English.

Example: 'Go straight along and then turn left.'

READING FOR INFORMATION 4 JOURNEYS

Reading for Information
4. JOURNEYS

When Rosa got to Finchley Road station, she bought an Underground map. She travelled south on the Jubilee Line, and got off the train at the fifth station, which was Green Park. Rosa had to change lines at Green Park. She got on a westbound Piccadilly Line train. On the train she counted the stations again. She got off at the third stop, which was South Kensington.

Follow Rosa's journey from Finchley Road to South Kensington on this London Underground map:

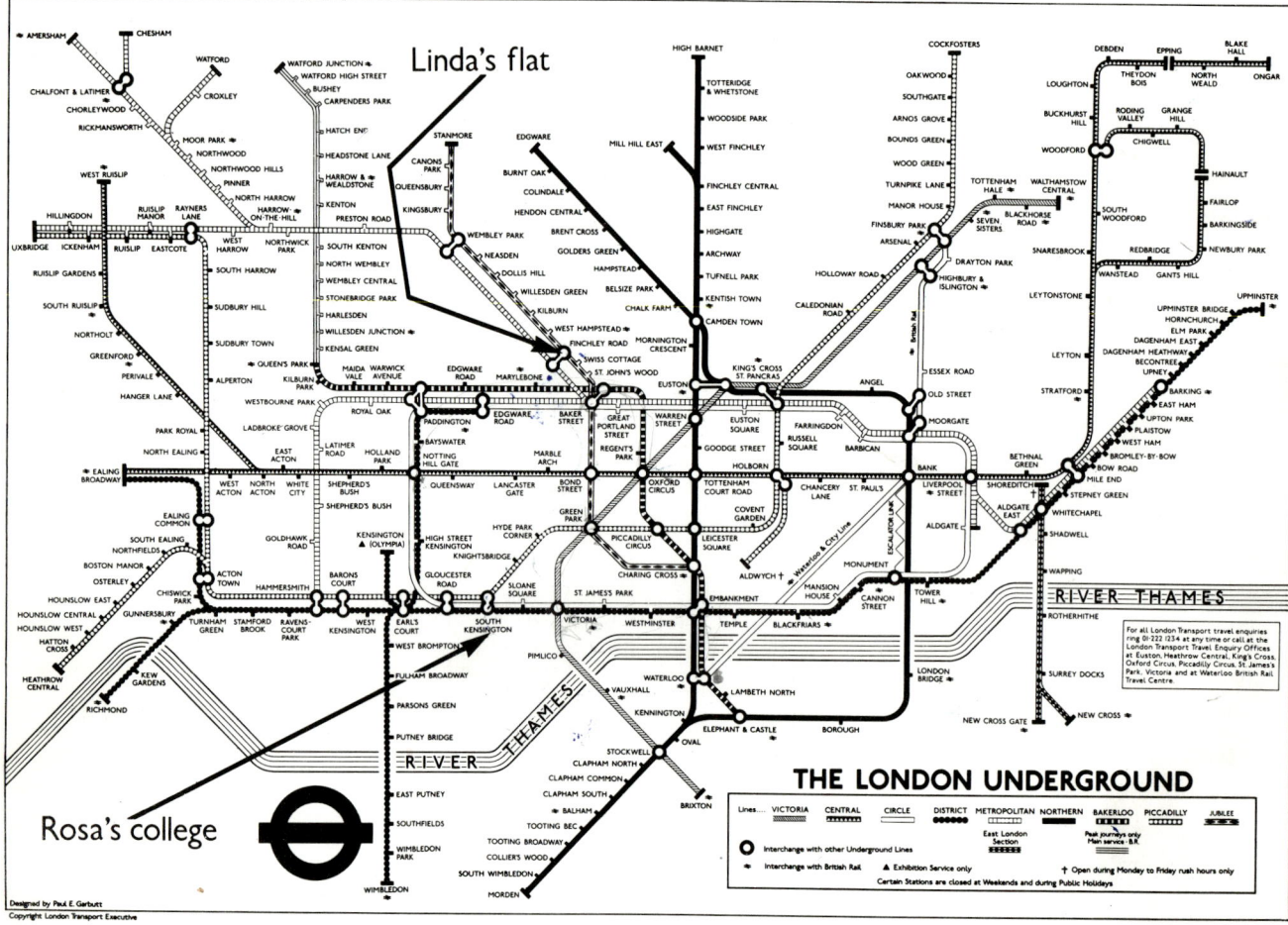

LINE	SYMBOL	COLOUR	OTHER SYMBOLS
Bakerloo		brown	stations
Central		red	
Circle		yellow	
District		green	change to other underground lines
Jubilee		grey	
Metropolitan		purple	change to British Rail overground trains
Northern		black	
Piccadilly		dark blue	the River Thames
Victoria		light blue	

READING FOR INFORMATION **4 JOURNEYS**

1

①

1 Rosa counted the stations, because she was worried about getting off the train at the right station. When the train stopped at the stations, Rosa could only see **part** of the place names.

Which station was Rosa at when she saw:

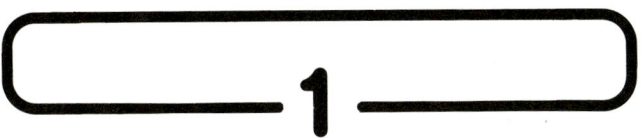

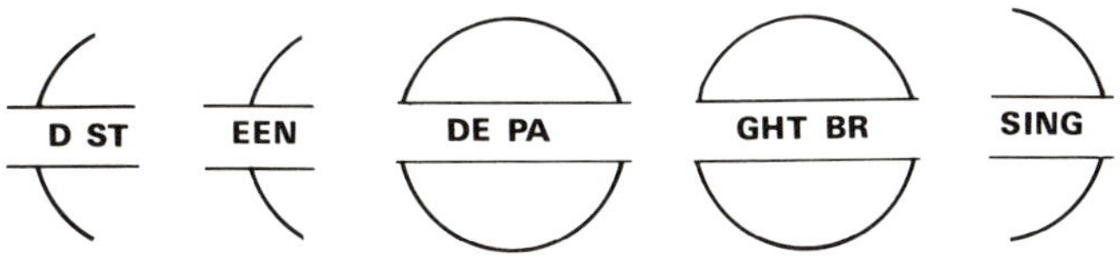

2 Rosa found the Underground map easy to read. Each line was a different colour.

What colour are these lines?

Piccadilly   Bakerloo   Victoria   Northern Central

3 Rosa travelled first on the Jubilee Line. Finchley Road is on the Jubilee Line and also on the Metropolitan Line.

Which line, or lines, are these stations on?

Knightsbridge   Regent's Park

South Kensington   Paddington

4 To go from Finchley Road to South Kensington, Rosa had to change lines at Green Park.

Where do you change for these journeys?

South Kensington to Waterloo

Piccadilly Circus to Victoria

Finchley Road to Heathrow

5 London is divided into north and south by the River Thames.

Are these stations north or south of the river?

Waterloo   Baker Street   Richmond

South Kensington

② The map uses SYMBOLS. Look at these directions:

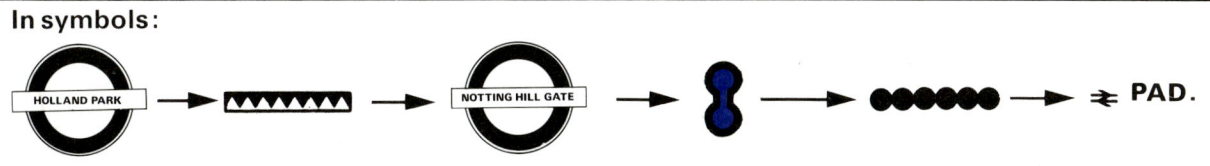

'From Holland Park station, take the Central Line to Notting Hill Gate. Then change to a District Line train for British Rail Paddington.'

Can you change these symbols into words?

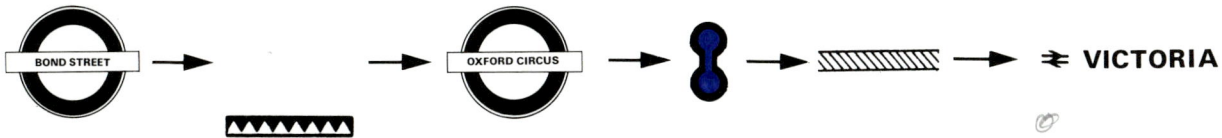

③ How quickly can you read this, changing the symbols into words?

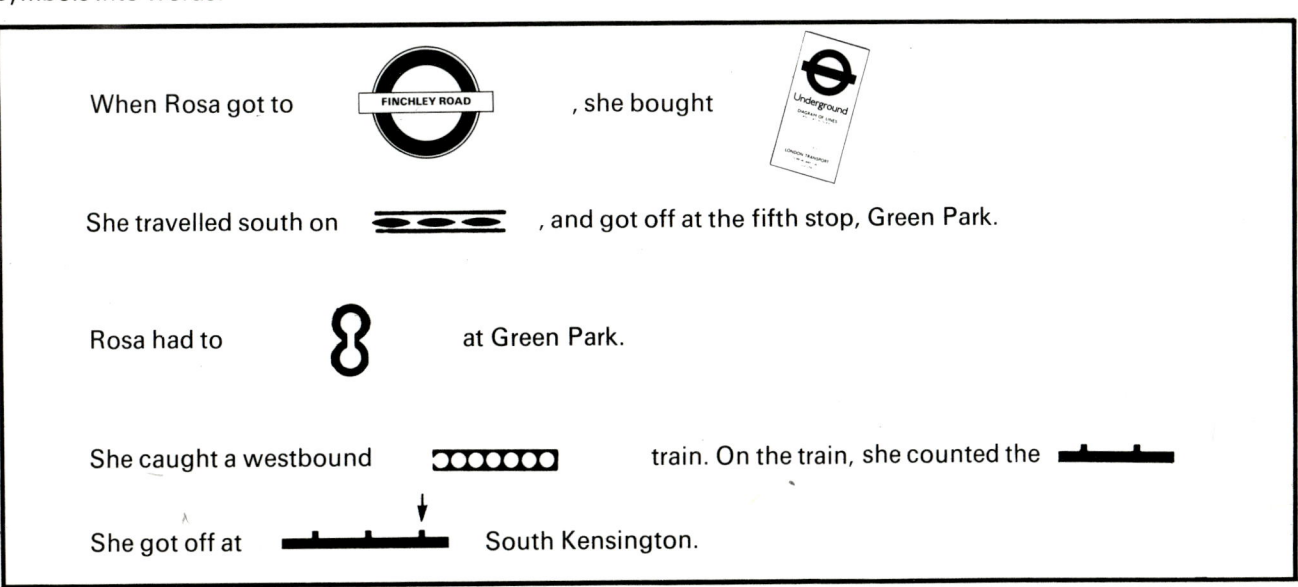

15

READING FOR INFORMATION 4 JOURNEYS

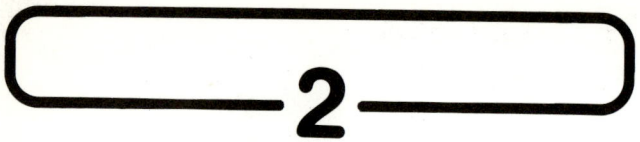

This is a page from a hotel GUIDE BOOK.

① Read the symbols and their meanings:

② Here is the entry for the Hotel Concorde, Paris.

It means:

The Hotel Concorde in Paris is a good hotel. The telephone number is 88-66-21. It is in the city centre.

The hotel is open all year and there are forty bedrooms. There is central heating in the hotel.

Breakfast is from seven to nine, lunch is from eleven to three, and dinner is from eight until eleven. There are twenty-five bathrooms and fifteen showers. There is also a swimming pool in the hotel. The nearest railway station is two kilometres away.

Now read these symbols, and describe the hotels in the same way:

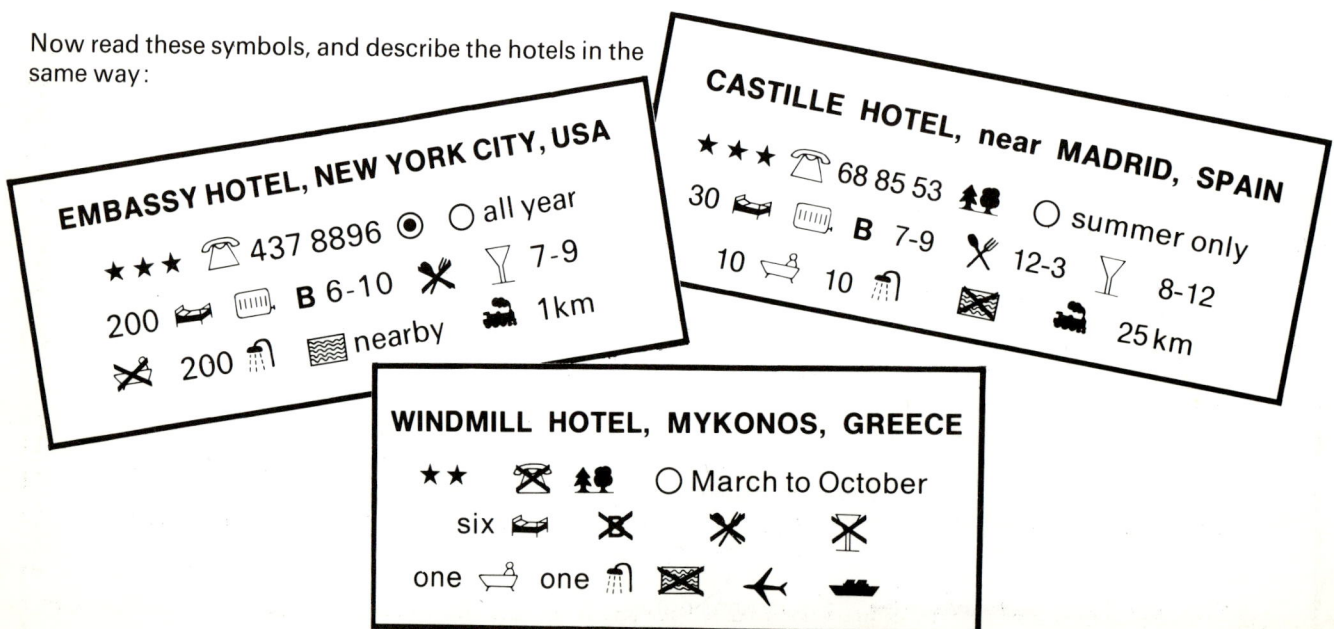

READING FOR INFORMATION **4 JOURNEYS**

3

① A friend of yours is travelling from Paddington to Exeter. Use the British Rail Timetable to get information.

Ask and answer questions, like this:

A Is there a restaurant on the 11.30 train?
B Yes, there is.
A Is there a 20.30 train on Fridays?
B No, there isn't.

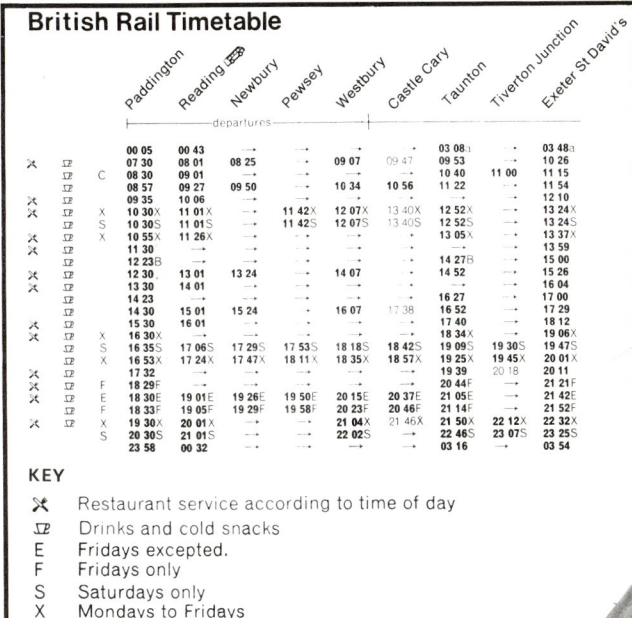

② How quickly can you match these symbols with the words in the right column:

      There is a station in the city centre

You can park your car

You cannot park your car

   Medical attention (First Aid)

Women's Lavatory

Men's Lavatory

    Railway line

Camping near a wood

Church

      Take care. Children crossing the road

Men working

The road narrows

skills check

You have read: **An Underground Railway map**
An Overground Railway timetable
A Hotel Guide Book

You have practised: **1 Reading symbols for information.**

Example: 'There's a good hotel in the city centre.' ★★★★ ◉

2 Changing symbols into words.

Example: the third station

3 Guessing meaning from situation.

Example: 'It must be Hyde Park.'

17

READING FOR INFORMATION 5 NOTICES

Reading for Information
5. NOTICES

When she got to Pembroke College, Rosa found a lot of people there. She wondered what to do and where to go. At first, she stood with a lot of other students in front of the college notice-board. Then she decided to ask the young man standing next to her for help.

Rosa	Excuse me. Can you help me please? I'm a new student and I want English classes.
Carl	So do I.
Rosa	Oh! Are you a foreign student, too?
Carl	Yes. I'm Swedish. You're Spanish, aren't you?
Rosa	No. I speak Spanish, but I come from Colombia.
Carl	Well, I think we both go to GENERAL ENQUIRIES ROOM 102.
Rosa	But what about ROOM 110 NEW FIRST YEAR STUDENTS? We are both new first year students.
Carl	Yes you're right... No, wait a minute. Let's look at the whole list first...
Rosa	What about ROOM 290 ENGLISH LANGUAGE? Do you think that's right?
Carl	No, look, further down, near the bottom... ENGLISH FOR FOREIGNERS NEW AND OLD STUDENTS.
Rosa	That sounds right. What does EFL stand for?
Carl	English as a Foreign Language, I think.
Rosa	That's it!
Carl	O.K. Let's go to Room 310. By the way, my name is Carl, Carl Lindstrom.
Rosa	I'm Rosa. Rosa Morello.
Carl	I'm glad we met, Rosa.
Rosa	So am I, Carl.

Notice Board

```
Pembroke College           Enrolment Day

ALL GENERAL ENQUIRIES         Room 102
Hotel Management                   103
Business Management                104
Science Courses (DAY)              106
Science Courses (NIGHT)            107
NEW FIRST YEAR STUDENTS            110
Geography                          203
History                            207
French                             237
German                             264
Spanish                            276
OTHER FOREIGN LANGUAGES            281
English Language                   290
English Literature
Engineering (DAY)                  292
Engineering (NIGHT)                293
English For Foreigners             310
(EFL NEW AND OLD STUDENTS)
Accountancy                        296
Drama                              294
Art                                311
Pottery                            357
Yoga                               381
ALL OTHER COURSES                  390
```

18

READING FOR INFORMATION **5 NOTICES**

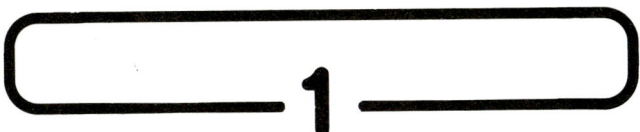

① Tick the two correct facts about Carl and Rosa:

They are	old students	
	new students	
	English Language	
	Foreign Languages	
	English as a Foreign Language	

② Complete this sentence about Carl and Rosa. Use the words:

English   language   as   both   They

...... are ...... students of ....
a Foreign ......

③ Both Carl and Rosa made a mistake. They both read slowly down the list of subjects and rooms, instead of quickly reading the whole list first.

What was the first word at which Carl stopped reading?

What was the first word at which Rosa stopped reading?

④ Carl and Rosa are students of English as a Foreign Language. They enrol in Room 310.

Where do these students go?

Meena	a second year accountancy student
David	a third year student of Spanish
Tina	a student doing a second year Science course in the evening
Maria	a third year History student
Paul	a student from another college looking for his sister
Mick	a degree student in his first year at the college
Laura	a housewife interested in yoga
Yoko	a photography student
Barbara	a drama student
Graham	a student of Russian

⑤ The room for EFL students to enrol in is on the third floor.

Which floor are these rooms on?

Business Management
General Enquiries
Pottery
Chinese
daytime Science courses
Architecture
Art
German
evening Engineering courses
Hotel Management

⑥ Carl wants a **full-time** course in **technical** English.

Rosa wants a **part-time** course in **general** English.

The relevant words for Carl are –
full-time and **technical**.

The relevant words for Rosa are –
part-time and **general**.

In Room 310, they were given this notice:

```
   NOTICE TO STUDENTS      EFL
 Please enrol on the correct form
 Course                                Form
 Part-time course in English conversation   A
 Full-time course in general English        B
 Part-time course in general English        C
 Part-time course in spoken English         D
 Full-time course in written English        E
 Full-time course in technical English      F
 Part-time course in technical English      G
```

Which form does Carl want?

Which form does Rosa want?

READING FOR INFORMATION 5 NOTICES

2

JOB ADVERTISEMENTS

① Choose a word pair from the list below.

Then, as quickly as possible, **scan** the job advertisements.

Do not try to read everything. Just look for the words relevant to you.

When you find the job which fits your two words, read the advertisement carefully.

Example:

Your word pair is:

part-time — Kensington

Stop and read this advertisement.

Word Pairs

part-time	languages
full-time	South Kensington
money	cars
part-time	typist
secretary	hospital
restaurant	evening
EFL	teacher
college	technical

General Jobs

Medical secretary and receptionist urgently required for doctors in busy hospital. Perm. or temp. F/T or P/T. Telephone 930 0279

Publishing secretaries (Permanent and Temporary) – it's always the widest choice at our agency. Reply Box No. 428.

ASSISTANT FILM EDITOR
Speaking German or French for the production of language courses. Full or part-time job. Telephone for appointment 606 0374

● **PART-TIME** evening work available in busy, friendly restaurant. Would suit student. Kensington area. Phone Richard 01-892-1704 after 6pm.

● Are you a good teacher? Part-time work available (day or evening) for experienced teachers of EFL. Send for application form to School of Languages, The College, St Mary's Rd. Ealing. W5.

● **FLAT CLEANING WORK AVAILABLE** Mornings/afternoons £3 + fares per 4 hour sessions. 289 1310

● **We need a responsible secretary** with commercial experience. Ability to type **TECHNICAL** mss. an advantage. The job is part-time (2½ - 3 days) at £8.50 per day. Please write as soon as possible to UNITED WRITERS, 30 North View, London SW14.

● **Accurate typist** 50 wpm for Third World news agency. Five days a week plus alternative Saturdays. **GOOD MONEY** for the right person. Ring 624 0321.

● **PART-TIME** youth worker for Adventure Playground in Paddington area. £18-£27 for approximately 12 hour week. Male preferred to balance female influence. Write to Brenda. Box No. 436.

● **HAVE** you got technical qualifications? **DO** you like variety? **CAN** you work under pressure? Small, busy, friendly college requires audio/visual aids technician urgently. Apply in writing to N.C.I.L.T. Recreation Road, Southall, Middlesex.

● **WANTED.** Car park attendants. Must be first class drivers with experience of wide range of vehicles. Hours 42 per week including shift work, and opportunity for overtime. Full pay during training. Telephone for details and application form to 580 0929 (24-hour answering service).

GOOD MONEY
for efficient people. We need more owner/drivers for our expanding circuit. 4-door CARS, MINIS, VANS or MOTORBIKES.
Phone Jake 947 0293.

YOUNG PERSON required to work as clerk/typist in museum, situated South Kensington. This is a full-time job (Hrs. 10-6) with training and good prospects. Salary on scale £2,341 - £2,593. Tel. 584 0739.

Good typist, 3 days a week. Salary by arrangement. Ability to handle a small switchboard an advantage. Box No. 24.

P/T hardworking, cheerful and efficient typist needed by LITERARY AGENT with a bad temper. Salary negotiable. Telephone for appointment (not before 10.30 a.m.). 01-351 1921.

COLLEGE EXAMINATIONS UNIT
For the attention of all students:

1. Examinations start on June 16th. and finish on July 7th.
2. Morning examinations begin at 9.30a.m.
3. Afternoon examinations begin at 2p.m.
4. All examinations last three hours.
5. The college closes at 5.30p.m. each day during examinations.
6. Examination fees must be paid before June 1st.
7. No student can enter the examination room more than 15 minutes after the beginning of an examination.
8. No dictionaries or other reference books may be used.
9. No smoking is allowed in examinations.
10. No one may leave the room in the last thirty minutes of an examination.

② Here is a LIST of rules about examinations:

A student who smokes will find point 9 on the list relevant.

Which point (or points!) are relevant to these people?

A student who wants a holiday in June.

A student who does not have much money.

A student who likes to study in the college in the evening.

A student who is always late!

A student whose last bus leaves at 5 p.m. each day.

READING FOR INFORMATION 5 **NOTICES**

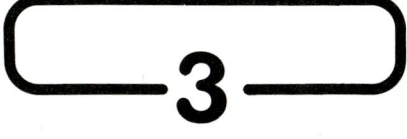

1 Your friend is visiting a hospital. Use the hospital notice-board to get information about where to go. Ask and answer questions, like this:

Where do I go for a prescription?

Room 2, ground floor west.

Where do new patients go?

Room 1, ground floor east.

Where is the Maternity Ward?

Room 5, on the first floor.

HOSPITAL GUIDE

GROUND FLOOR

WEST ←
- Room 1 Admissions
- Room 2 Prescriptions
- Room 3 Hearing Aids
- Room 4 Eye Tests
- Room 5 Blood Tests

EAST →
- Room 1 New Patients
- Room 2 Out Patients
- Room 3 Bank
- Room 4 Cafeteria
- Room 5 X-Ray

FIRST FLOOR
- Room 1 Social Workers
- Room 2 Hospital Secretary
- Room 3 Children's Ward
- Room 4 Old People's Ward
- Room 5 Maternity Ward

AIRLINE	FLIGHT NUMBER	DESTINATION	DEPARTURE TIME
BA	384	Sao Paolo	10:01
SAB	486	Paris	10:07
BA	902	Zurich	10:18
LH	612	Stuttgart	10:26
PAN AM	786	Los Angeles	10:30
KLM	332	Madrid	10:35
SAB	604	Paris	10:41
KLM	622	Amman	10:55
KLM	801	Stockholm	10:58
LH	205	Delhi	11:00

2 Get information from this Airport Departures notice-board, by reading quickly up and down columns, across rows, and by reading letters, numbers and times.

1 How many British Airways flights are there?

2 Where is flight 604 going to?

3 Which airline is flying to Amman?

4 Which flight takes off at 10.58?

5 How many different destinations are there?

6 How many planes take off between 10.25 and 10.45?

7 Where is the Pan Am flight going to?

8 When does flight 902 take off?

9 How many different airlines are there?

10 When does the flight for Stuttgart take off?

skills check

You have read: **Notices**...... in a college, in a hospital, in an airport.

Lists...... of courses and rules.

Advertisements...... for jobs.

You have practised: **1 Scanning** – reading quickly up, down and across.

2 Looking for relevant information.

Example: 'I'm a new student of E.F.L.'

READING REVISION 1

① **How quickly can you match these pairs?** Match each TEXT (**A-Q**) with its DESCRIPTION (**1-17**).

Example: **A-5** is a correct pair – An alphabetical index.

Box	Description
8	A chart
1	A letter
H	Jan.
10	Telephone
16	A shopping list
5	An alphabetical index
3	A form
6	A grid map
12	A book title
17	A question
15	A job advertisement
9	No Left Turn
14	A passport photograph
11	A guide
4	Number sixty-nine
2	The abbreviation for January
7	A London address
13	The abbreviation for south-west one

Texts shown include:
- **K**: Personal Information Chart (Surname SCHORN/BAUM, First Name Heinz/Sabine, Sex Male, Age 14, Height (metric) 1.58)
- **P**: PART-TIME youth worker for Adventure Playground in Paddington area. £18–£27 for approximately 12 hour week. Male preferred to balance female influence. Write to Brenda. Box No. 436.
- **F**: (photograph of bearded man)
- **O**: (door with number 69)
- **L**: (No left turn sign)
- **G**: Arkers FLOOR GUIDE — BASEMENT: Kitchen Ware, Electrical Goods; GROUND: Gloves, Handbags, Perfumery, Haberdashery; FIRST: Ladies Fashions, Hats, Shoes; SECOND: Childrens Wear, Ladies Hairdressing; THIRD: Men's Wear, Linen; FOURTH: Furs
- **I**: Mr J Robinson, 24, St. Peters Street, London, SE10 8JG
- **Q**: OAD SW1
- **C**: (map of Spain with grid, showing Santander, Bilbao, Valladolid, Zaragoza, Barcelona, Tarragona, Madrid, Toledo, Valencia, Cartagena, Malaga, Almeria)
- **N**: (telephone symbol)
- **B**: The Director, Pembroke College, Pembroke Road, London, W.8. — Stockholm, Sweden, April 20 — Dear Sir/Madam, I am coming to London in the summer to improve my English. Please send me an form for your English
- **D**: ?
- **M**: INTERNATIONAL STUDENT TRAVEL — SURNAME MORELLO, SEX, ADDRESS, FIRST NAMES, NATIONALITY, AGE, TELEPHONE, HEIGHT, Attach p
- **E**: 5 lbs of potatoes, 2 lbs of sugar, 4 lbs of apples, Tea, Coffee, Salt, Dog Food
- **J**: (books including THE SKY IS MINE by T. Hunt)
- **A**: Penhall Rd. SE7 – 4B 66 / Penhill Rd. Bex – 1D 101 / Penistone Rd. SW16 – 1F 107 / Penketh Dri. Harr – 4D 23 / Penmon Rd. SE2 – 4C 68 / Pennack Rd. SE15 – 1D 79 / Pennant M. W8 – 4F 59 / Pennant Ter. E17 – 4E 19 / Pennard Rd. W12 – 3C 58 / Penn Clo. Gnfd – 3C 38 / Penn Clo. Harr – 1A 26 / Penner Clo. SW19 – 2D 91 / Pennethorne Clo. E9 – 3F 47 / Pennethorne Rd. SE15 – 2E 79 / Penn Gdns. Chst – 2E 113

READING REVISION 1

② How quickly can you use an alphabetical index?

1 These are the London telephone directories. Names beginning with **F** are in **E-K**.

What about names beginning with:

M   T   C   G   O   U   I   Q   Z

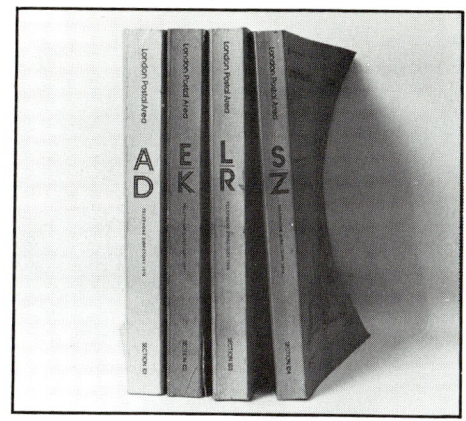

2 You are looking in the directory for the name **Newlyn**.

This page	421 Newman, D LONDON POSTAL AREA Newman, J 421	is too far.
This page	419 Newham LONDON POSTAL AREA Newland 419	is not far enough.
This page	420 Newland LONDON POSTAL AREA Newman, D 420	is right!

What about these:

For **Shah**   Shaw is..

For **Smith P**   Smith N is..

For **Robinson D**   Robins is...

For **Hussein**   Inman is..

For **Higa**   Hill is..

③ How quickly can you solve these letter puzzles?

1 These are the names of some countries in South America.
One of them is where Rosa comes from. But the letters are in the wrong order, and the countries are in the wrong place on the map.

How quickly can you:

find the countries.

put them in alphabetical order.

put them in the correct place on the map.

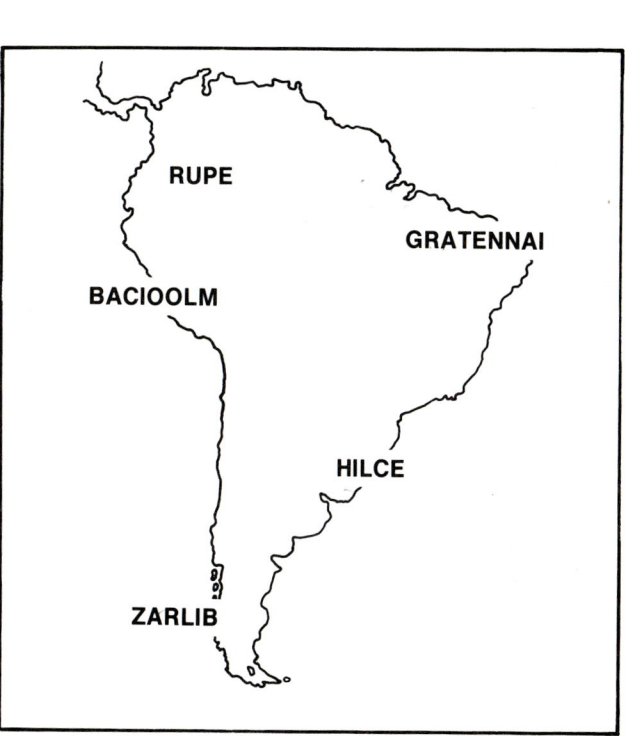

READING REVISION 1

2 This is a crossword puzzle.

Read the clues and find the missing words in the **Reading for Information** section.

Clues

ACROSS

1 You can find Linda's ...... on her form (7)

4 You can check your measurements on the ...... on p. 5 (5)

5 An abbreviation for 'morning' (2)

7 On p. 13 there is a ...... of a museum (4)

8 On p. 3 you filled in a ...... for Rosa (4)

9 On p. 10 Linda told Rosa to ...... left (4)

10 What is the ...... for a good hotel? (6)

14 To find Pembroke Road, Linda looked in the A-Z ...... (5)

15 Rosa and Carl had to ...... at a notice-board (4)

16 In letters 10 is ...... (3)

DOWN

2 You drew a ...... on p. 11 (7)

3 To find how far Zurich is from Berne you read a ...... on p. 12 (5)

6 Rosa bought a ...... of the Underground (3)

7 You need a ...... or a pencil to follow Linda's directions on p. 11 (3)

10 Which direction was Rosa's college from Linda's flat? (abbreviation) (2)

11 You will usually find the index in the back of a ...... (4)

12 At Pembroke College there was a ...... of subjects and rooms (4)

13 To read the weather map on p. 9 you had to use the ...... (3)

SECTION 2
Reading for Meaning

READING FOR MEANING 1 INSTRUCTIONS

Reading for Meaning
1. INSTRUCTIONS

Rosa and Carl filled in ENROLMENT FORMS. ▼

Here is Rosa's form.

```
PEMBROKE COLLEGE
Department of English as a Foreign Language
Enrolment Form C            EFL 672/2/C
```

USE BLOCK CAPITALS

1. Name   ROSA   MOrELLO
   (underline family name)

2. Title (underline)   MR/MRS/<u>MISS</u>/MS/OTHER

3. Nationality   COLOMBIAN

4. London Address   144A CANFIELD GARDENS
                     LONDON nW6

5. Telephone number   I do not remember it

6. Do you need help with accommodation?
   (circle 'yes' or 'no')   YES   (NO)

7. I have studied English
   (tick as appropriate)   (a) less than 1 year
                           (b) 1 - 2 yrs
                        ✓ (c) 2 - 5 yrs
                           (d) more than 5 yrs

8. On which days can you NOT come to class?
   (please delete)

   Monday - Tuesday - Wednesday - Thursday - ~~Friday~~

9. Do you prefer classes
   (tick as appropriate) ✓(a) in the mornings
                           (b) in the afternoons
                           (c) in the evenings

10. SIGNATURE   Rosa Morello

FOR OFFICE USE ONLY

Enrolled for class Elementary   Full-Time/(Part-Time)

Fees Paid   by cheque/(in cash)

Student Ref. No. EFL/86324   EFL/80/C

READING FOR MEANING 1 **INSTRUCTIONS**

1

① Look at the INSTRUCTIONS on Rosa's form.
Rosa has followed the instructions correctly.

For example:

Students must **use** block capitals:

Students must **underline** their family name:

Students must **circle** the answer to question 6:

② Now look at parts of Carl's form. It is the same form as Rosa's.
Has he followed the instructions correctly?
For example:

(underline)

correct ⟶ MR/MRS/MISS/MS/OTHER

What about these?

(tick as appropriate)

1 (b)✓ 1 - 2 yrs

(tick as appropriate)

2 (a)✓ in the mornings

(please delete)

3 day - (Tuesday) - Wednesday -

4 London Address SOLÖVÄGEN 2 OSKAR FREDERICKS STOCKHOLM, SWEDEN

5 Name CARL LINDSTRÖM
(underline family name)

③ Now answer these questions about Rosa. The answers are on her form.

When you are writing your answers, follow the instructions in brackets about how to answer the questions.

1 What is Rosa's family name? (use block capitals).

2 Rosa is   male   female   (underline).

3 Which country does she come from? (use block capitals).

4 Does Rosa have a telephone?

YES   NO   (circle correct answer).

5 Does she need help with accommodation? (write Yes or No).

6 On which days can Rosa come to classes (tick as appropriate).

Monday   Tuesday   Wednesday   Thursday   Friday

7 How long has Rosa studied English?
(tick as appropriate)

a six months   b three years   c seven years

8 When does Rosa not want to come to classes? (delete).

a in the mornings   b in the afternoons
c in the evenings

9 Which class has the college enrolled Rosa for? (underline).

Elementary / Intermediate / Advanced

10 How did Rosa pay her fees (underline).

by cheque / in cash

READING FOR MEANING 1 INSTRUCTIONS

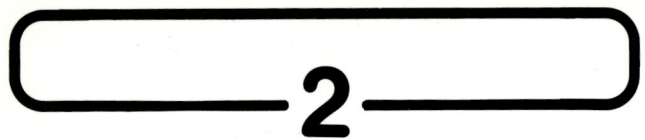

① Paul Williams is an American. He is going to Europe on vacation. Read his BOOKING FORM: ▼

Europeamerica Tours				**Vacation Booking Form**		
Please write clearly USE BLOCK CAPITALS						
NAME (underline surname)	PAUL <u>WILLIAMS</u>					
ADDRESS	428 STATE STREET ATHENS, OH10, USA					
Tel. No.	(614) 688-9102					
Cities			**Persons No.**	**Rooms**		
Which will you visit?				Type	No.	Bath (CIRCLE)
City	No. of nights	Adults	2	Single		YES NO
Amsterdam						
Athens	2	Children (3 - 14 yrs)	2	Twin (1 rm. 2 beds)		YES NO
Florence	3					
London	4					
Madrid		Infants (under 3 yrs)	1	Double (1 rm. 1 bed)	1	**YES** NO
Munich						
Paris	2					
Rome				Triple (1 rm. 3 beds)	1	YES **NO**
Venice						
Zurich						
YOUR ACCOMMODATION COSTS				**CHARGES** (accommodation only)		
Per night: Adult(s)		$60		Each adult : $30 per night		
Child(ren)		$40		Each child : $20 per night		
Bathroom(s)		$10		Each bathroom : $10 per night		
Total per night		$110		Infants : FREE		
Total no. of nights		11		N.B. Fares are separate		
TOTAL ACCOMMODATION COST		$1210				
I enclose a deposit of $121				SIGNED Paul Williams		

② Answer these questions about Mr Williams' form:

1 How many children under 14 years old is Mr Williams taking?

2 How many rooms does Mr Williams want each night?

3 How long will Mr Williams stay in England?

4 How much would the accommodation cost without the children?

5 How much does Mr Williams still owe Europeamerica Tours?
(Remember he has paid a deposit.)

③ Copy out the form, and fill it in for:

MARGARET STOCKER

She lives at 1444 Riverside Drive, San Francisco, California. Her telephone number is (415) 882 3142. She will be travelling alone, and she wants a single room with a bath every night. She will be visiting Amsterdam for two nights, London for six nights, Munich for one night and Paris for four nights.

DAVID MORRIS

He lives at 2824 East 44th St., New York, New York. His phone number is (212) 998 6745. He will be travelling with his mother and his two children (ages 13 yrs and 2 yrs). They will be visiting Florence for three nights, Rome for four nights and London for seven nights. Each night Mr Morris wants two single rooms (both with bath), and one double room without bath.

READING FOR MEANING 1 **INSTRUCTIONS**

3

Here is a QUESTIONNAIRE. ▼

You can use it to make a survey of the people in your class or school, or at home with your family and friends.

QUESTIONNAIRE ABOUT LEISURE TIME.

NAME ....
(use block capitals)

SEX (circle)   MALE   FEMALE

Do you like............?

Indicate with a cross   (X)

Activity	YES	NO
playing sports		
watching sports		
going to the theatre		
going to the cinema		
going to concerts		
eating out		
watching television		
listening to pop music		
other activities: fishing		
cycling		
walking		
talking		

Please write in any other interests
....
....
....

① Write out copies of this questionnaire. Ask different people to fill it in. Then answer these questions:

1 How many people filled in the questionnaire?
2 Which activity is the most popular?
3 Which activity is the least popular?
4 How many females answered?
5 Which activity is most popular with females?
6 Which activity is least popular with females?
7 How many males answered?
8 Which activity is most popular with males?
9 Which activity is least popular with males?

② Now put your answers on this SURVEY FORM. ▼

LEISURE TIME – RESULTS OF SURVEY

No. of forms   ....
No. of females   ....
No. of males   ....
MOST POPULAR   (all) ....
                    (F) ....
                    (M) ....
LEAST POPULAR (all) ....
                    (F) ....
                    (M) ....

RESULTS (Write YES or NO)
Males and females have
the *same* interests ....
Males and females have
different interests ....

skills check

You have read: **A form** ...... for enrolling in classes.
                     ...... for booking a holiday.

A questionnaire ...... for a survey of leisure time.

You have practised: **1 Reading instructions.**

Examples: use (block capitals) COLOMBIAN   delete   Y̶E̶S̶/NO
            underline   YES/<u>NO</u>   indicate YES ☐ NO ☒
            circle   YES/Ⓝ̶Ⓞ̶   (with a cross)
            tick   YES ☐ NO ☑   write   No!

2 Reading English titles.

Examples: Mr = a man   Mrs = a married woman
            Ms = a woman   Miss = an unmarried woman

3 Reading abbreviations often used on forms.

Examples: Tel. no. = telephone number   Ref. no. = reference number
            M = male   N.B. = Nota Bene = read carefully
            F = female

READING FOR MEANING 2 MESSAGES

Reading for Meaning
2. MESSAGES

At eleven o'clock that morning, Linda telephoned Pembroke College. Linda wanted to speak to Rosa. The switchboard operator answered the call.

Operator	Good morning. Pembroke College. Can I help you?
Linda	Yes please. I want to speak to a student. Her name is . . .
Operator	I'm sorry. I'm afraid nobody can speak to students today. It's enrolment day. The college is very busy.
Linda	Oh dear! Well, can you take a message?
Operator	Well, we *are* very busy . . .
Linda	Oh *please!* It's very important.
Operator	Well, O.K. I'll take the message. I hope it's short!
Linda	Thanks. She's a foreign st . . .
Operator	Just a minute. Now, who is the message *for?*
Linda	Rosa Morello. That's M-O-R-E-double L-O.
Operator	Thank you. And who is the message *from?*
Linda	Say 'Linda'. I'm her flatmate.
Operator	Yes. And what is the message *about?*

Linda	It's very important. Please tell her *not* to go back to the flat.
Operator	'Don't go back to the flat.' Yes?
Linda	Tell her I've bought some theatre tickets.
Operator	'Theatre tickets.' Yes?
Linda	Tell her to be at St Martin's theatre.
Operator	'St Martin's'. Yes?
Linda	At seven o'clock tonight.
Operator	'Seven o'clock'. O.K. I'll write this . .
Linda	Oh wait. Just a minute. I nearly forgot. Tell her to bring someone with her. I've got *four* tickets.
Operator	'Bring someone'. Is that all now?
Linda	Yes, thanks. Rosa is a foreign student. She's enrolling for English classes.
Operator	Thank you. I'll write out the message and send it to the EFL department.
Linda	Thanks very much. 'Bye.
Operator	Goodbye. I hope you enjoy the play.

READING FOR MEANING 2 MESSAGES

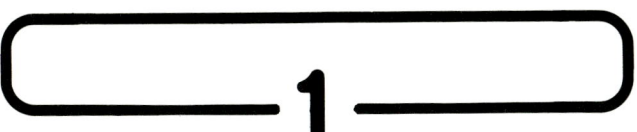

① Answer these questions about Linda's message:

1 What has Linda bought?
2 Where must Rosa go?
3 What time must Rosa be there?
4 What does Linda tell Rosa to do?
5 What does Linda tell Rosa not to do?

② Now look at these two different versions of Linda's message:

These are the short notes the operator made when she was talking to Linda.

This is the complete message the operator wrote for Rosa and sent to the EFL Department.

```
Mess. 11-00 a.m.
ROSA MORELLO
      fr. flatmate LINDA
- v. imp.
- don't go back flat
- L. has bt. th. ticks.
- be at St. Mart's th. 7 p.m.
- br. s.o.
- 4 ticks           EFL
```

```
PEMBROKE COLLEGE    MEMOS/MESSAGES
TO: Ms. R. Morello   FROM: Linda
Date: Sept. 14th    Time: 11 a.m.
SUBJECT:
   There was a phone call this morning from
your flatmate Linda. She said the message is
very important.
   She said don't go back to the flat. She
has bought some theatre tickets. She wants you
to be at St. Martin's Theatre at 7 o'clock tonight.
She said bring someone with you, she's got
four tickets.

          Department: E.F.L.
```

③ Look at the operator's short notes. She has missed out some words.

She has also made some words shorter.

For example:

Mess = message

fr. = from

Here are some more abbreviations:

bt.	th.
Mart's	imp.
ticks.	7 p.m.
s.o.	L.
v.	br.

What are the ten complete words in the long message?

④ Look at the operator's complete message.

She has put in all the words missing from the notes.

For example:

'from your flatmate Linda'.

The word 'your' is in the message, but **not** in the notes.

Which words in these sentences are in the message but not in the notes?

'the message is very important'.

'don't go back to the flat'.

'she has bought some theatre tickets'

'She wants you to be at St Martin's theatre at seven o'clock tonight'.

'she said bring someone with you'.

'she's got four tickets'.

31

READING FOR MEANING 2 MESSAGES

2

Helen is married to a business-man and has a small son. Sometimes Helen's husband has to travel from London. Helen likes to go with him when she can. Her parents live near her and always look after the little boy when his mother is away.

One day Helen visited her parents, but they were not at home. Helen was in a hurry, so she wrote a note and pushed it under the door.

① Read Helen's message and look for her abbreviation of these words:

**something   weekend   business trip
please   Edinburgh**

Helen has made her message shorter by:

1 missing out some words — 'I' from the beginning of sentences.

some short words like 'at', 'on'.

For example:

'Thought you'd be home.'

I thought you'd be **at** home.

2 using some common abbreviations

For example:

a.m. – morning

Fri. – Friday

3 using some of her own abbreviations

For example:

w.e. – weekend

pl. – please

> Dear M!
> Came early this p.m. just after 1. You weren't in! Thought you'd be in. Are you and D. out shopping?
> Wanted to ask you s.th. Can you pl. look after David this w.e.? Am going with Mike on bus. trip to Edin. (Fri. eve – Sun. p.m.) And D. wants to stay with grandm. and grandad again! Hope you are both well.
> Love H.
> P.S. Almost forgot — will bring D. Fri. p.m.

② You know that Helen is married, has one son and is going on a business trip with her husband.

Use this information to guess the answers to these questions:

1 Who is 'M'?
2 Who is 'grandm.'?
3 Who is the first 'D' in the message?
4 Who is the second 'D' in the message?
5 Where will Helen be on Saturday?
6 What is the name of Helen's husband?
7 What does 'eve' mean?
8 P.S. means 'Postscript'. When is it used?

③ Write out Helen's message in full. Put in all the missing words, and write abbreviations in full.

Begin:

I came early this afternoon, just .....

④ Here is a note from Helen's husband. Put these missing words into the right places:

on   the   to   at   I

```
Take David * your parents * Friday
afternoon. Meet me * * station *
4.30p.m. * train goes * 5p.m. * will
be in * waiting room * platform 1.
         Love,
         M.
```

READING FOR MEANING 2 MESSAGES

3

① This is an English Dictionary ENTRY.▼
Can you find abbreviations for:

noun   somebody   something   slang

> **mess·age** /ˈmesɪdʒ/ n **1** piece of news, or a request, sent to sb: *Radio ~s told us that the ship was sinking. Will you take this ~ to my brother? Got the ~?* (sl) *Have you understood?* **2** sth announced by a prophet and said to be inspired social or moral; teaching: *the ~ of H G Wells to his age.* **mess·en·ger** /ˈmesɪndʒə(r)/ n person carrying a ~.

What is ~ a symbol for?

② This is a message in full. Can you make it shorter by using abbreviations for:

people   places   times   dates

```
Dear David,
    Your friend John telephoned
at half-past nine this morning.
He wanted to tell you that he
will be at the Central Square
cinema next Tuesday evening at
seven o'clock. He asked me to
tell you not to be late.
        Michael.
```

③ This is a TELEGRAM.▼

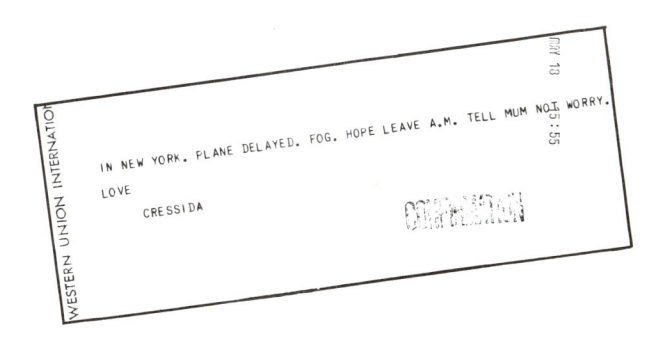

> WESTERN UNION INTERNATIONAL
> IN NEW YORK. PLANE DELAYED. FOG. HOPE LEAVE A.M. TELL MUM NOT WORRY.
> LOVE
>   CRESSIDA

Below is the same message in a telephone conversation.▼

Can you put the information below in the same order as it appears in the telegram?

Begin: 'I'm in New York.'

'Tell Mum not to worry about me.'

'because of the fog.'

'I'm in New York.'

'My plane is delayed'

'I hope to leave in the morning.'

skills check

You have read: **Informal notes** ...... from a telephone call.   *L. has bt.*

                               ...... between relatives.   *Take David * your afternoon. Meet me*

                Formal messages ......   MEMOS/MESSAGES FROM: ...Linda.   *Dear David, Your friend Joh*

                A telegram ...... **words** are missed out to make the message shorter.

                A dictionary entry ...... **letters** are missed out to make the entry shorter.

You have practised: **1 Reading notes**
                     by recognizing common abbreviations.
           Example: phoned a.m. = telephoned in the morning
                     by guessing other abbreviations.
           Example: You know Linda phoned Rosa, therefore 'L' = Linda
                     by putting in missing words.
           Example: Meet me station 4.30 p.m. = Meet me at the station at 4.30 p.m.
                     2 Guessing meaning from situation.
           Example: You know Helen is at her parents' home, therefore Dear M = Mother (or Mum)

READING FOR MEANING 3 FACTS

Reading for Meaning
3. FACTS

After enrolling Rosa and Carl looked at the student notice-board. It had a lot of POSTERS, NOTICES, ADVERTISEMENTS and MESSAGES on it.

Student Union Notice Board

ENTERTAINMENT

DISCO
ALL WELCOME
[especially new students]
This Saturday 9p.m.–12p.m.
Green Common Room
Admission £1
Late Bar: Drinks till 12p.m.
Tickets: Union Office

ACCOMMODATION

Available now! (girl only)
1 Sunny room in large flat for four.
Share kitchen and bath
Only £9 p.w. – includes hot water and TV!
Contact Maggie – Student Union Office

WANTED – Please help.
Language student (male) wants single room, near College.
About £10 per week
Tel: 01-373 0029

SPORT

FOOTBALL ON SATURDAY
Sorry! No match – not enough players

JOBS

JOBSJOBSJOBSJOBSJOBSJOBS
Dino's Italian Restaurant
(just around the corner)
want a part-time (evenings)
waiter/waitress
Good money! Free food!

HELP THE HOMELESS
Thousands of people in this city are homeless. They have nowhere to live, nowhere to sleep.
Many of these people are students.
You can help!
– by giving money
– by giving your time
– by giving us the names and addresses of other people who can help

Write, call or phone:
Help The Homeless
27 West Street
London W8

Metropolitan Police
Crime Prevention Advice

BEWARE Pickpockets

They're after your:
* Wallets
* Purses
* Credit cards

DON'T LET THEM GET AWAY WITH IT!

34

READING FOR MEANING 3 FACTS

1

① Look at (don't read!) the notices and posters quite quickly. They all use different kinds of writing:

large print — **HELP THE HOMELESS**

small print — **Many of these people are students.**

handwriting — *not enough players*

Which poster uses all three kinds of writing?

② Now read the notices and posters more carefully. They give information about

    time — Saturday 9 p.m.–12 p.m.
    place — Green Common Room
    cost — Admission £1

1 What time does the Disco bar close?
2 When will the waiter/waitress work?
3 Where does the language student want a room?
4 What's the address of Help the Homeless?
5 How much is the room for a girl student?
6 How much will the waiter/waitress pay for food?

③ Now think about the subject of each notice or poster. They each have a different purpose.

Find a notice or a poster which:

says sorry	—	this is an **apology**
tells students to be careful	—	this is a **warning**
asks for help	—	this is a **request**

④ Read the notice (right) and the poster (left), and label the kinds of writing, the information and the purpose for each one. There are some examples to help you.

ENGLISH SOCIETY THEATRE VISIT

ANNUAL TRIP TO :

STRATFORD-UPON-AVON

This year we are going on Nov.16th to see:

MACBETH

The £15 cost includes
fare - ticket - meals - tips

Coaches leave college at 10 a.m.
DON'T BE LATE! - WE WON'T WAIT !

Soon! £3 deposit please to:
Anne Francis

P.S. I am sorry we couldn't get tickets for Hamlet — all sold out. A.F.

Information
- subject ☑ (arrow to SPORT)
- date ☐
- time ☐
- place ☑ (arrow to STRATFORD-UPON-AVON)
- cost ☐

Purpose
- request ☐
- apology ☑ (arrow to P.S.)
- warning ☐

Kinds of writing
- small print ☐
- large print ☐
- handwriting ☑ (arrow to P.S.)

SPORT

International Soccer
ENGLAND v. W.GERMANY
We now have tickets
(£7 each)
PLEASE *pay now.*
for the match at
WEMBLEY
Nov. 1st.
Kick - off
Apologies! 8 p.m.
7.30 p.m.
P. Grey
Soccer Sec.
Student Union

REMEMBER:
You must bring your union cards. No card - No ticket!

35

READING FOR MEANING 3 FACTS

Read these posters and notices.

Film Festival
6 – 19 Feb

Blacks in the Cinema
The New Western
Tribute to Jack Nicholson
Documentary Student Films
Young Cinema

Sixty premiers Over 100 films
All night film shows Dances
Discussions with film makers

Details : Festival Office
Thames Polytechnic
Thomas Street Woolwich
London SE18 6HU
01 855 0618

Thames Film Festival
6-19 Feb

Richmond Shakespeare Society

AS YOU LIKE IT

by William Shakespeare

February 6th.–11th. at 7·45

Cardigan Hall Theatre
Petersham Road, Richmond

Tickets 75p & 50p

BOX OFFICE
8 Hill Court, Putney SW15 .... 01- 789 2200
Marian Jardella
57 Albert Road, Richmond 01- 948 0043

LOST !!!
Please help! I have lost 2 tickets for the film festival (Feb 18th) I think I left them in Lecture Theatre I yesterday between 2-3. If you find them, please _please_ ring me (evenings)
Babs Rabin Phone 788 2196
(Grosvener House Student Hostel) Jan 21st

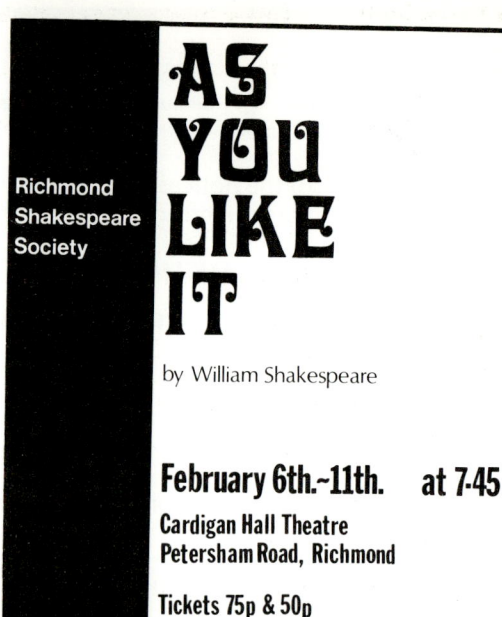

SPECIAL NOTICE

AS YOU LIKE IT Theatre Visit (Feb 5) Will students please collect and pay for tickets before Feb 1.
Tickets not paid for will not be kept I will send them back to the Theatre.

Aileen Gross
Senior Lecturer in English Literature
Rm 213

Jan 20th

2

① The Film Festival

Read the whole of this telephone conversation first. Then, look back at Babs Rabin's note on this page. You can then complete the missing part of this dialogue.

Babs Hello, Babs Rabin here.
You ....
Babs Oh good! When did you find them?
You ....
Babs The morning? But I _had_ them in the morning. Where did you find them?
You ....
Babs In Two? But I lost them in LT1! How many did you find?
You ....
Babs Four? For the seventeenth? Oh dear, they are _not_ mine!
You ....
Babs You could put a message on the notice-board. I did!

READING FOR MEANING 3 FACTS

② As You Like It This is a true statement about the poster: Tickets cost £1.

This is a false statement about the play: It begins on February 5th.

Look at each of these statements and say whether they are True or False.

	True	False
1		
2		
3		
4		
5		
6		
7		
8		
9		
10		

1 *As You Like It* is by William Shakespeare.
2 This production is by the Richmond Theatre Company.
3 The Box Office number is 789-0043.
4 The play is on for six nights.
5 Each performance begins at a quarter to eight.
6 Students must pay for their tickets before February 5th.
7 Six tickets cost £6.
8 Aileen Gross is in Room 20.
9 Uncollected tickets will go to the theatre.
10 There is a mistake on Aileen Gross' notice.

3

Make a notice or a poster, in English, to advertise an event in your school, college or neighbourhood.

1 Use different kinds of writing:
block capitals/small print/handwriting.

2 Give clear information:
about dates/time/place/cost/subject.

3 Include one of these:
a request/a warning/an apology/a welcome.

skills check

You have read: **Posters**   advertising ...... A Film Festival
                                                A play
                                                A Disco

Notices   requesting ...... WANTED — Please help.

apologizing ...... Sorry! Apologies!

warning ...... DON'T BE LATE! - WE WON'T WAIT

You have practised: **1 Reading information**
Examples: date ... on February 6th – 11th
            time ... at 7.45 p.m.
            place ... at Cardigan Hall Theatre
            cost ... Tickets £1

2 Identifying subject   SPORT   THEATRE VISIT

3 Recognizing kinds of writing.
Examples: ...... **LARGE PRINT**
            ...... Small Print
            ...... handwriting

4 Answering True/False questions

READING FOR MEANING 4 OPINIONS

Reading for Meaning
4. OPINIONS

Next, Carl and Rosa looked at some pictures in a college corridor. The pictures were the work of students in the college Art department. Sometimes Carl and Rosa agreed about the pictures, but sometimes they disagreed.

Rosa I like this one. It's terrific.

Carl So do I. I love pictures of mountains. ▼

A MOUNTAIN SCENE — 3rd YEAR

Carl I don't like this one. ▶
Rosa Don't you? I think it's good.
Carl Good? It's terrible, Rosa.
Rosa Oh, I disagree. It's super.

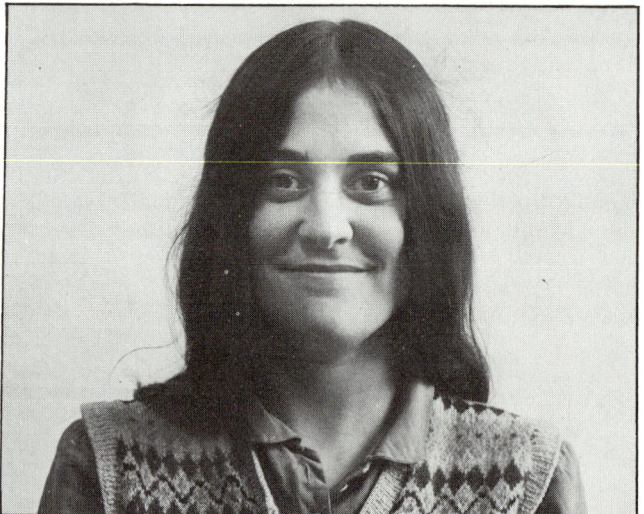

Photograph of my friend — 2nd YEAR

◀ **Rosa** What about this one?
Carl I don't like portraits.
Rosa Nor do I. It's awful.
Carl Mm! She looks terrible.
Rosa I agree. I think so too. Poor girl!

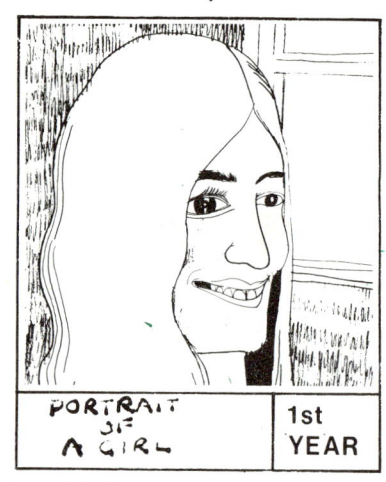

PORTRAIT OF A GIRL — 1st YEAR

Rosa Dreadful!
Carl Dreadful? It's sensational!
Rosa I don't agree. I hate abstract paintings. It's really bad.
Carl Oh, I like abstracts. I think it's the best painting here.
Rosa Do you? I think it's the worst!

▶ Painting with no title — 3rd YEAR

READING FOR MEANING 4 OPINIONS

1

① Do these quotations from the text express liking or disliking?

'I like this one.'

'I hate abstract paintings.'

'I love pictures of mountains.'

'I don't like portraits.'

② Sometimes Rosa and Carl agree. Sometimes they disagree. Do these quotations from the text express agreement or disagreement?

The speaker	said	agreement	disagreement
Rosa	Don't you?		✗
	Nor do I.		
	I think so too.		
	I don't agree.		
Carl	So do I.		
	Good?		
	Mm!	✗	
	Dreadful?		

③ Which three of these words express a similar 'good' opinion?

terrific   awful   super   sensational

Which three of these words express a similar 'bad' opinion?

terrible   dreadful   good   awful

④ Read the text and find opposites for:

I hate   I like   bad   the best

⑤ Look at the table below. How many true statements can you make now? ▼

Rosa	likes	the mountain scene.
Carl	doesn't like	the photograph.
Both Rosa and Carl	like	portraits.
Neither Rosa nor Carl	likes	abstract paintings.
Rosa and Carl	agree about	
	disagree about	

⑥ Use some of the words on this page to complete these conversations:

Agreeing

A I like the portrait

B ...... do I.

A I ...... the abstract.

B Nor do I.

A I ...... abstracts.

B I agree.

Disagreeing

A I like the photograph, it's good.

B Do you? I think it's ......

A I don't like the portrait, it's awful.

B ...... you? I think it's good.

A I think the mountain scene is super.

B ...... ? It's terrible!

⑦ Now have a conversation with a friend about one of the pictures. Like this:

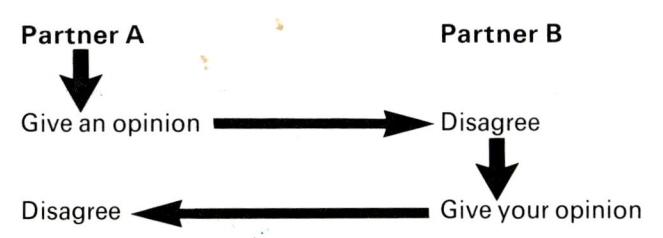

Partner A — Give an opinion → Partner B — Disagree → Give your opinion → Disagree

39

READING FOR MEANING **4 OPINIONS**

Read this Opinion Page from a magazine. ▼

IN YOUR OPINION

Hello again!

Last week I wrote about the subject of TV violence. I gave you my opinion. I also wrote about the opinions of two American professors – experts on the subject of TV and violence.

In the last week, many of you have written to me with your opinions. Here they are:

SHOULD YOUNG CHILDREN SEE PROGRAMMES LIKE THIS?

T.V. Violence

```
Dear Editor,
     I agree with you. The experts are right!
There is too much violence on T.V. There
are too many programmes about crime, war
and death. I hate them. They are awful.
I never watch them.
     Violence on T.V. is definitely bad for
children. My son and his friends watch
American programmes. Then they play very
violent games, where they pretend to kill
each other.
     These games are terrible. I am sure that
T.V. violence causes a lot of today's crime.
               Yours sincerely,
               J. Freshney (Mrs), Yorks.
```

Dear Editor,
   About TV Violence, I don't agree with you. And I think that the 'experts' are wrong. Violence on TV teaches kids about life. Some of those American programmes are very realistic.
   My daughter and I love those programmes. We always watch them. They are super! And we are very peaceful people! They should show more action programmes. They're great!
   I think a lot of today's crime is caused by bad parents, not by TV.
   Sincerely,
   (Mrs) P. Hickson, Wembley, London

Photographs from two British TV programmes.

More letters on page 3.

READING FOR MEANING 4 OPINIONS

2

① Read the letters from Mrs Freshney and Mrs Hickson.

Who **likes** American programmes?

Who **dislikes** American programmes?

Who **agrees** with the Editor of the magazine?

Who **disagrees** with her?

② Mrs Freshney uses the word **awful**. Find another word in her letter that expresses the same opinion.

Mrs Hickson uses the word **super**. Find another word in her letter that expresses the same opinion.

③ In her letter, Mrs Freshney uses the words:

death   hate   never   right   violent

Read Mrs Hickson's letter, and find five words with opposite meanings.

④ Do you think the Editor likes violent TV? Give a reason.

Do you think the Editor agrees with the experts? Give a reason.

3

① Read these two letters to a London newspaper.

Which writer liked the Dylan concert?

Which writer disliked the Dylan concert?

② Complete the two sentences about Miss Marks and Mr Watkins. Use these words:

beautiful   crowded   expensive

friendly   peaceful   uncomfortable

1 Miss Marks liked the concert because Dylan was . . . and the fans were . . . . . . She thought the concert was very . . . . . .

2 Mr Watkins disliked the concert because it was too . . . . . ., and he was . . . . . . He did not see or hear Dylan because it was too . . . . . .

LETTERS

DYLAN: Not seen or heard.

I READ your review of the Dylan pop festival with some interest. In my opinion, it was the worst buy in the history of music. I paid £6 to sit cramped and paralysed on a flat airfield. It was so crowded I saw and heard nothing. I used to enjoy pop festivals but I was cured last Saturday. Never again!
K. Watkins, Birmingham.

I WRITE this letter to all those people who can't understand the fuss about Bob Dylan's concert. His music is unique and he is the poet of our generation. There was a strong feeling of friendship at his concert. While Dylan sang everyone was holding hands. Complete strangers were talking to each other. Bob Dylan was beautiful and so were his fans. He brought us together for two and a half hours. That's what all the fuss was about.
R. Marks (Miss), London.

skills check

You have read: **The Opinion Page of a magazine.**

Letters expressing agreement and disagreement.

Letters expressing liking and disliking.

You have practised: **1 Reading opinions**

Examples: . . . . . . agreeing – I agree with you.

. . . . . . disagreeing – I don't agree with you.

. . . . . . similar – good – terrific – beautiful – best

. . . . . . opposite – bad – terrible – awful – worst

2 Reading different reasons for opinions

. . . . . . it is bad for children.

. . . . . . they are very realistic.

. . . . . . his music is unique.

41

READING FOR MEANING 5 PERSUASION

Reading for Meaning
5. PERSUASION

At lunchtime, Carl and Rosa were hungry. They found a restaurant near the college and stopped outside to read the MENU. It looked very good.

The Lettuce Leaf
Are you hungry?

Do you want fresh food at fair prices?

Then why not come inside and enjoy good food, and fast, friendly service at a cool, quiet table.

MENU

May we suggest . . .
START with a plate of one of our famous fresh salads.
Choose from – beef, chicken, ham, soft Cheddar cheese.
All served with a great green salad and ripe red tomatoes.
Choose from – large, extra large, mountain-size!

WITH YOUR MEAL, why not have . . .
a basket of freshly-baked bread
a glass of wine.
Choose from – cool white or rich ruby red.

THEN why not try . . .
our famous fresh fruit salad?
FINISH with a cup of hot fresh coffee
Choose from –
large or small
black or white

Everything at The Lettuce Leaf is made on the same day as you eat it.

The Lettuce Leaf – famous for the freshest food at the fairest prices.

WHY NOT COME AGAIN?

Inside The Lettuce Leaf, Carl and Rosa sat down and waited. They waited for a long time. At last a waiter came.

Waiter Yes?

Rosa I want a cheese salad please.

Waiter Large, extra large or mountain-size?

Rosa Er–large please.

Waiter Anything else?

Rosa Yes. I'll have some bread, a glass of white wine and a small cup of white coffee.

Waiter (to Carl) What's yours?

Carl A chicken salad – mountain-size. And with it I'd like bread, white wine and a large black coffee please.

READING FOR MEANING **5 PERSUASION**

Carl and Rosa waited another ten minutes. Then their food arrived.

Carl Mountain-size! But I've only got a small piece of chicken, one tomato and a few pieces of lettuce!

Rosa This Cheddar cheese is very hard.

Carl So is the bread!

Rosa I know. It's not fresh at all, it's stale. I can't eat it.

Carl And I can't drink this wine. Cool? It's warm!

Rosa Terrible! And there's no cream in my coffee.

Carl But there is in mine! And it's cold. Where's the waiter?

Rosa I don't know. Perhaps he's gone to lunch in another restaurant!

1

Carl and Rosa were persuaded to eat at The Lettuce Leaf by the language used in the menu.

① The menu uses a lot of words with 'good' meanings.

Examples:

good food – not **bad** food

fast service – not **slow** service

Find five words with 'good' meanings and five with 'bad' meanings:

fresh   great   friendly   terrible   soft

stale   hard   rude   quiet   unfriendly

Now use some of the words to say what was wrong with the lunch:

Example:

Carl's salad was not large, it was small.

What was wrong with:

Carl's coffee?   Rosa's cheese?
The bread?   The wine?   The service?

② The menu also uses a lot of words about the same SUBJECT.

Example:

small, large, extra large, mountain are all about size.

How many words are there about the subject of colour?

How many times is the word 'fresh' used?

Which of these words is not about the subject of food or drink:

tomato   salad   ripe   price   baked   fruit

Which of these words is not about things which hold food and drink:

glass   basket   plate   cool   bowl   cup

③ The menu also uses a lot of words with the same sound.

Example:

The sound 'f' is used five times in:

'**f**amous **f**or the **f**reshest **f**ood at the **f**airest price'

How many times is the sound 'b' used in:

'a basket of freshly baked bread'

What sound is used to describe:

the tomatoes?   the red wine?   the fruit salad?

④ The menu also uses:

questions   – 'are you hungry?'

suggestions   – 'why not come inside?'

instructions   – 'start with ......'

Say whether these sentences are questions, suggestions or instructions:

1 May we suggest a plate of salad.

2 Do you want fresh food at fair prices?

3 Why not have a glass of wine?

4 Choose from large or small.

5 Finish with a cup of hot fresh coffee.

6 Why not try our fresh fruit salad?

7 Why not come again?

READING FOR MEANING 5 PERSUASION

Britain's most famous marmalade. Thick, rich, chunkily chewable. Dark with the unmistakeable aroma of Seville oranges. From Oxford it was carried around the world to the Antarctic, the Americas, even Everest itself. And became a part of the great tradition of the British breakfast.

FRANK COOPER'S "OXFORD" Coarse Cut MARMALADE 454g 1lb

FRANK COOPER makes the marmalade that makes the British breakfast.

▲ ADVERTISEMENTS ▶

EXCURSIONS BY TRAIN & SHIP
Sail Away to France, Holland and Belgium
Summer
UP TO 48 HRS ON THE CONTINENT

Here's a chance to enjoy a short trip with a difference at very modest cost. A short while after leaving England you can be on the Continent in an atmosphere which is delightfully different. During the crossing you can shop on board at attractive prices. The savings alone can make your trip even more worthwhile.

There are through bookings from London and selected stations. Ask for the Sail Away brochure, giving full details, at British Rail Travel Agents, principal British Rail stations or travel offices.

Sealink

2

① **The advertisement for Frank Cooper's 'Oxford' marmalade**

1 'Oxford' is the name of a place. How many other place names can you find?

2 How many times is the word 'marmalade' used?

3 How many times is the phrase 'British breakfast' used?

4 Say the words 'Britain's most famous marmalade'. How many times did you say the sound **'m'**?

5 Here are five words from the advertisement. Find three with 'good' meanings.

part   great   famous   breakfast   rich

② **The Sail Away advertisement**

Read the whole advertisement, but do not try to understand every word:

What is advertised?   How do you travel?
Where can you travel?   How long can you stay?

How many words about the subject of money can you find?

The advertisement suggests four reasons for making this trip:

1 enjoyment   2 low cost   3 interest in life abroad
4 shopping tax-free at low prices

Look at the illustration. Which reason does British Rail think is the most important?

BARBADOS is the most beautiful of the West Indian islands. The blue Caribbean sea laps the white sand in front of the **MIRAMAR BEACH HOTEL.**

At the Miramar you will find friendly service. Our staff are eager to make your visit the most enjoyable vacation ever. You can swim, or just lie in the sun on our glistening white sand beach. Then why not have a cool, tropical cocktail at our beach bar …

from ……. A HOTEL BROCHURE ▲

BARBADOS is the most easterly of the islands in the Caribbean sea. It is served by the world's airlines and is within easy reach of Montreal, New York and London.

There is a mild tropical climate (80–85 degrees).

The island is hilly, but not mountainous. The highest point is near the centre of the island (1104 ft.)

The island is surrounded by safe, sand beaches.

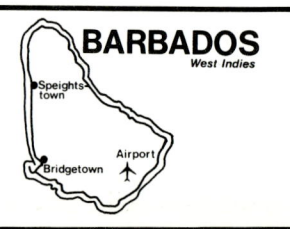

BARBADOS West Indies
Speightstown
Bridgetown
Airport

from ……. A GUIDE BOOK ▶

READING FOR MEANING **5 PERSUASION**

③ Look at the pages from the guide book and from the hotel brochure about Barbados.

1 Look at the ILLUSTRATION in each text.
Which illustration gives **information**?
Which illustration tries **to persuade**?

2 Look at the **first sentence** in each text.
In which text does the first sentence give an **opinion**?
In which text does the first sentence state a **fact**?

3 Now read both texts quite quickly.
Which words does each text use to describe the **beach(es)**?
Which words does each text use to describe the **sea**?

4 Now look for the word 'tropical' in each text.
In which text does 'tropical' describe a **drink**?
In which text does 'tropical' describe the **weather**?

3

① Write an advertisement in English.

You can use an illustration.

Repeat words or sounds.

Choose words with 'good' meanings.

Use different words about the same subject.

② Write a letter of complaint to The Lettuce Leaf from Rosa.

skills check

You have read: **A menu** ...... from a restaurant.
A Guide Book ...... for the island of Barbados.
A hotel brochure ...... for a Barbados Hotel.
Advertisements ...... for food and travel.

You have practised: **1 Reading the language of persuasion.**

Examples: questions ...... Are you hungry? / Do you want ...?
suggestions ...... you can shop / why not try / you will find
instructions ...... choose from / start with ...

2 Recognizing word groups.

words with the same subjects ...... colour – green / blue / white / red
words with 'good' meanings ...... young – not old / soft – not hard

3 Recognizing the use of repetition.

same words ...... fresh food / fresh salad / fresh bread
same sounds ...... British breakfast / rich ruby red

4 Recognizing the use of illustration.

READING REVISION 2

Read this story **twice**.

Read it very quickly the first time. Then read it again more carefully.

THE PARCEL

Last week a friend stayed at my flat.
She arrived from Switzerland on Tuesday morning,
and she left London on Thursday evening.

She wanted to do some shopping on Thursday
morning. Before I went to work, I left her a   5
message. I told her to meet me at half-past
five, at the newspaper stand, at Gloucester
Road station. Then I would carry her luggage
and shopping to the Air Terminal.

I arrived at the station on time.   10
I went to the newspaper stand. There were
lots of people at the station. At first,
I could not see Marie. I put my briefcase
down. Then I heard Marie's voice.
'Hello Dave!' she said.   15
'Hi Marie!' I answered. 'We can walk to the
Air Terminal from here.'

I picked up her shopping. It was
a big parcel. It was wrapped in brown paper.
It was also very heavy!   20
'Can you carry my briefcase, Marie?' I asked.
'Of course,' said Marie. 'Let's go!'

We walked down the street. It was
very busy. The traffic was very noisy.
'The traffic's terrible,' said Marie.   25
'Yes, awful!' I shouted.
'It's very kind of you to help me, Dave,'
said Marie.
'Oh that's all right Marie,' I said,
'I've only got my briefcase.'   30
'But your parcel looks very heavy!' said
Marie.

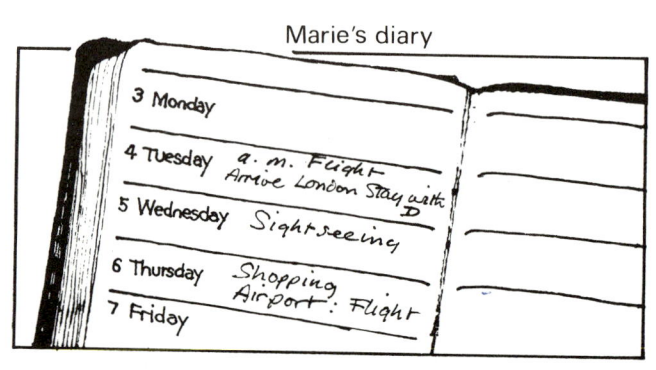

Marie's diary

3 Monday
4 Tuesday a.m. Flight
Arrive London Stay with D
5 Wednesday Sightseeing
6 Thursday Shopping
Airport: Flight
7 Friday

Dave's message

M
See you at Gloucester Rd. station
(newspaper stand) at 5.30 p.m.
I'll go with you to the Air Terminal.
It's nr. station. I'll help you with
your luggage and shopping
Love D

I stopped. '*My* parcel?' I said.
'It isn't my parcel. I thought it was
yours. I thought it was your shopping.' 35
'Oh no,' said Marie. 'I changed my mind.
I didn't do any shopping. I didn't have
time. It isn't my parcel Dave,' she said.
'Then whose parcel is it?' I said.
'I don't know!' said Marie. 40
We both laughed.
'Let's open it and look,' she said.

We opened the parcel. Inside,
there were fifty copies of a French
magazine. I had picked them up at the 45
newspaper stand! We both laughed again.

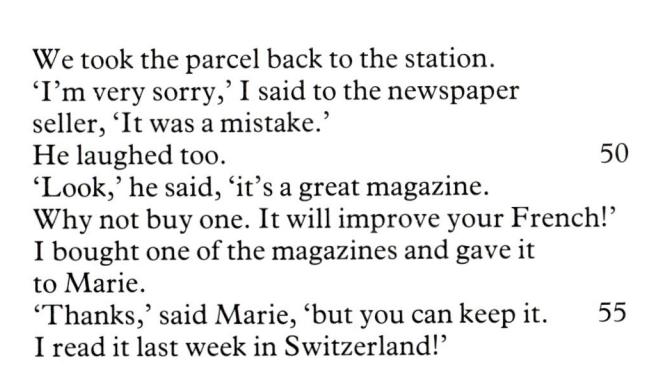

We took the parcel back to the station.
'I'm very sorry,' I said to the newspaper
seller, 'It was a mistake.'
He laughed too. 50
'Look,' he said, 'it's a great magazine.
Why not buy one. It will improve your French!'
I bought one of the magazines and gave it
to Marie.
'Thanks,' said Marie, 'but you can keep it. 55
I read it last week in Switzerland!'

Understanding **parts** of the story:

STEP 1 – Finding words and phrases

First, **scan** quickly.

Who said:

'Let's go!'

'We can walk.'

'I changed my mind.'

'Why not buy one?'

Then, **stop** and **look closely**.

Which lines do these quotations come from:

'Then whose parcel is it?'

'Yes, awful.'

'Can you carry my briefcase?'

'It's a great magazine!'

Where do these quotations come from:

It's nr. station

stay with D.

Understanding **parts** of the story:

STEP 2 – Recognizing language purpose

'Why not buy one.' in line 52 is an example of a **suggestion**.

Find an example of these:

an apology

a request

an abbreviation

an expression of agreement

an expression of opinion

READING REVISION 2

Understanding the **whole** story:
STEP 1 – Remembering details

Answer these questions without looking at the story:

Where did Dave and Marie arrange to meet?

Why did they arrange to meet?

What happened when they met?

How did Dave learn his mistake?

What did they do with the parcel?

Understanding the **whole** story:
STEP 2 – Order

Here are the events of the story, but they are in the wrong order.
How quickly can you put them in the right order:

They arranged to meet at the station.

They went back to the news stand.

They opened the parcel.

Marie arrived to visit Dave.

Dave waited near the news stand.

Dave picked up a suitcase and a parcel.

Dave apologized.

Marie said the parcel was not hers.

She had already read it.

He bought a magazine.

It was full of magazines.

He gave it to Marie.

Now use your answer to write the story in about 150 words, or tell it in about three minutes.

SECTION 3
Reading for Pleasure

READING FOR PLEASURE 1 PICTURE STORIES

Reading for Pleasure
1. PICTURE STORIES

After lunch, Carl and Rosa stopped at a newspaper stand. They wanted something to read. First, they looked at some COMICS.

Here are some words about comics:

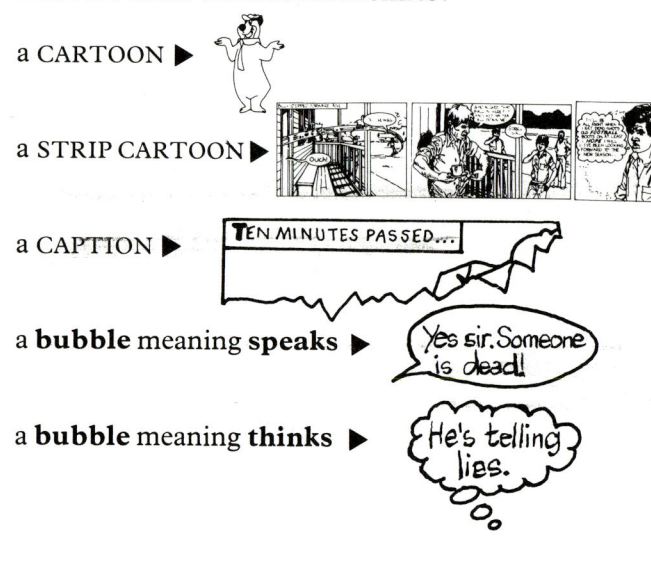

a CARTOON ▶

a STRIP CARTOON ▶

a CAPTION ▶ Ten minutes passed...

a **bubble** meaning **speaks** ▶ Yes sir. Someone is dead!

a **bubble** meaning **thinks** ▶ He's telling lies.

This strip cartoon is about a policeman called Mallet. He is investigating a robbery and a murder.

MALLET

THE KILDALE CASE

SOME GOLD AND SILVER JEWELS ARE MISSING. MALLET'S AGENT IS FOLLOWING SOMEONE...

Our agent thinks it is Lord Kildale, Superintendent.

Lord Kildale? Is she certain Mallet? He is one of my friends, you know.

Yes sir. She is. I must talk to Lord Kildale.

Yes, of course Mallet. This is terrible. Lord Kildale is a member of the Government.

LATER, MALLET GOES WITH HIS ASSISTANT, BRIGGS TO LORD KILDALE'S HOUSE

Yes sir. Someone is dead!

Look Briggs. That is Lord Kildale's house.

Who is she?

We don't know sir. A young woman. Blonde. About 25.

50

READING FOR PLEASURE 1 PICTURE STORIES

Did you know the dead woman Lord Kildale?

He had dinner with her last night.

He's telling lies.

Did you know the dead woman Briggs?

Yes of course Mr. Mallet. She was Delia Fish our agent!

Me? Know her? No!

LATER THE SUPERINTENDENT READS MALLET'S REPORT.

Well Mallet, you say that Lord Kildale has got the jewels! You think that he killed our agent.

Yes sir. That's right!

This is impossible, Mallet. I'm taking you off the Kildale case!

The superintendent doesn't want me to investigate. But WHY?

WHY IS THE SUPERINTENDENT TAKING MALLET OFF THE CASE?

WHAT DO YOU THINK?

1

① Choose the correct word in each of the sentences below.
The word is in the story.

Example:
Some gold and silver   coins / (jewels)   are missing.

1 Lord Kildale is a   (friend) / neighbour   of the Superintendent.
2 Lord Kildale is a member of the **police / Government.**
3 Briggs is Mallet's   **assistant / boss.**
4 The dead person is a young   **woman / man.**
5 Delia Fish was a police   **sergeant / agent.**

② Choose the correct word in each of the sentences below.
The word is not in the story.

Example:
Mallet is a   **criminal / (policeman.)**
(You know the correct answer because Mallett is investigating a murder and works with a superintendent.)

The Superintendent is   **happy / worried**   about the case.
Delia Fish was   **dark / fair.**
Mallett   **says / knows**   that Lord Kildale is lying.
The report says Kildale is a   **thief / politician.**
The report says Delia Fish's death was **murder / suicide.**
The Superintendent wants to   **stop / help**   Mallett on the Kildale case.

READING FOR PLEASURE 1 PICTURE STORIES

2

1 Here is another story, about a mountain accident. ▶
First, read the story without the words. Then, match the words below with the bubbles to tell the story.

- Help!
- Are you O.K.?
- I'm going for help.
- (Thinks) The rope . . .
- (Thinks) Will he be in time?
- No, I can't move. It's my leg.
- Please hurry.
- I'm falling.

At that moment, high up in the Austrian Alps...

After a long fall...

Ten minutes passed...

CONTINUED

2 Here is a strip cartoon without words. ▼
Look at the pictures and guess the words.
You could use:

a warning   **a question**   and **an apology**

Billy stepped forward. And...

Ouch!

READING FOR PLEASURE **1 PICTURE STORIES**

3

Look at this cartoon. ▶

This cartoon is from a COMIC called *Playland*.

It is for:

a little children ✓
b teenagers
c adults

It is from a story about:

a a murder
b a holiday
c a bird ✓

Now use the correct answers to write about the cartoon.

Example:

Playland is a comic for little children.
The cartoon is from a story about a bird.

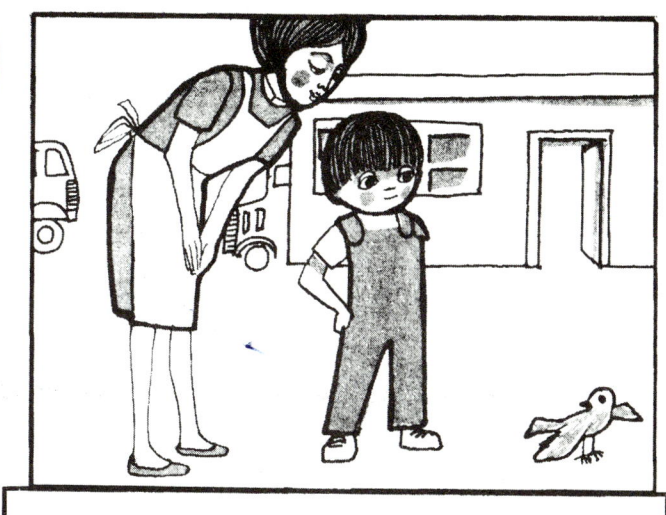

She came out to see. "Oh yes," she said. "It's a baby bird. It can almost fly but not quite."

Look at these cartoons and do the same.

① This cartoon is from a COMIC called *Judy*.

It is for:

a adults
b teenagers
c children

It is from a story about:

a crime
b war
c love

② This cartoon is from a NEWSPAPER called the *Daily Mail*.

It is for:

a business-men
b workers
c anyone

It is from an article about:

a cars
b politics
c holidays

③ This cartoon is from a MAGAZINE called *Star Wars*.

It is for:

a parents
b children
c everyone

It is from a story about:

a cooking
b skiing
c science-fiction

skills check

You have read: **Cartoons** ...... from comics.
　　　　　　　　　　　　　　　magazines.
　　　　　　　　　　　　　　　newspapers.

You have practised:
1 Reading pictures with words.
2 Using pictures to guess words.
3 Matching words with pictures to make a story.

53

READING FOR PLEASURE 2 MAGAZINES

Reading for Pleasure
2. MAGAZINES

Carl and Rosa decided to buy a magazine. They both liked pop music, and they both liked reading about people's lives.

So they bought a magazine called *Rock On*, and started to read the BIOGRAPHIES of a pop group called *Whitesnake*.

Rock On! BANDFILE No. 4: WHITESNAKE

NAME: David Coverdale
DATE OF BIRTH: 22 September, 1951
TOWN OF BIRTH: Saltburn-By-Sea
FIRST GROUP: Fabulosa Brothers/Deep Purple
INSTRUMENTS PLAYED: Guitar, keyboards and pink oboe
FIRST PUBLIC APPEARANCE: When I was five years old, on the teacher's desk I sang a medley of Tommy Steele hits.
WHERE DID YOU MEET THE REST OF THE BAND: David and Micky Moody were doing David's solo album, and the rest of the group joined by auditioning
INFLUENCES: Most old blues singers, like Robert Johnson, Muddy Waters, and Freddie King
FAVOURITE BAND(S): Little Feat
FAVOURITE SINGLE: Hey Joe—Hendrix
FAVOURITE ALBUM: Are You Experienced—Hendrix
WHERE DO YOU LIVE NOW: London

NAME: Neil Murray
DATE OF BIRTH: 27 August, 1950
TOWN OF BIRTH: Edinburgh
FIRST GROUP: Gilgamesh (jazz/rock)
INSTRUMENTS PLAYED: Bass
FIRST PUBLIC APPEARANCE: School dance, aged 15, played drums
WHERE DID YOU MEET THE REST OF THE BAND: Bernie Marsden contacted me
INFLUENCES: Cream, Tim Bogert and Jeff Beck, Stanley Clarke, Jaco Pastorius (Weather Report)
FAVOURITE BAND(S): Weather Report, Jeff Beck
FAVOURITE SINGLE: All Right Now—Free
FAVOURITE ALBUM: Hymn of the Seventh Galaxy, by Return to Forever
WHERE DO YOU LIVE NOW: London

NAME: David John Dowle
DATE OF BIRTH: October 20, 1953
TOWN OF BIRTH: London
FIRST GROUP: Streetwalkers, Brian Auger
INSTRUMENTS PLAYED: Drums
FIRST PUBLIC APPEARANCE: 1968—Croydon School, Muswell Hill, with Canterbury Glass Band
WHERE DID YOU MEET THE REST OF THE BAND: Auditioning
FAVOURITE BAND(S): Rufus
FAVOURITE SINGLE: All Right Now—Free
FAVOURITE ALBUM: Spectrum—Billy Cobham
WHERE DO YOU LIVE NOW: London

NAME: Michael Joseph Moody
DATE OF BIRTH: August 30, 1950
TOWN OF BIRTH: Middlesbrough
FIRST GROUP: Snafu, Young and Moody
INSTRUMENTS PLAYED: Guitar, slide guitar and mandolin
FIRST PUBLIC APPEARANCE: Saint Mary's Youth Club, Middlesbrough, 1965
WHERE DID YOU MEET THE REST OF THE BAND: I worked with David on his solo albums
FAVOURITE BAND(S): Little Feat
FAVOURITE SINGLE: Don't know
FAVOURITE ALBUM: Don't know
WHERE DO YOU LIVE NOW: London

NAME: Bernie Marsden
DATE OF BIRTH: May 7, 1951
TOWN OF BIRTH: Lancashire
FIRST GROUP: U.F.O.
INSTRUMENTS PLAYED: Guitar
FIRST PUBLIC APPEARANCE: High Wycombe, when I was 17
WHERE DID YOU MEET THE REST OF THE BAND: Through Micky Moody, I already knew him
INFLUENCES: Eric Clapton, Beatles, Jeff Beck, Joe Walsh
FAVOURITE BAND(S): As above, plus the Eagles
FAVOURITE SINGLES: Rocky Mountain Way—Joe Walsh
FAVOURITE ALBUM: John Mayall's Bluesbreakers
WHERE DO YOU LIVE NOW: London

DISCOGRAPHY:
ALBUMS
WHITESNAKE (TPS 3509) (PURPLE)
NORTHWINDS (TPS 3513) (PURPLE)
SINGLES
HOLE IN THE SKY (PUR 133) (PURPLE)
BREAKDOWN (PUR 136) (PURPLE)
SNAKEBITE (E.P.) (INEP 751) (SUNBURST)

READING FOR PLEASURE **2 MAGAZINES**

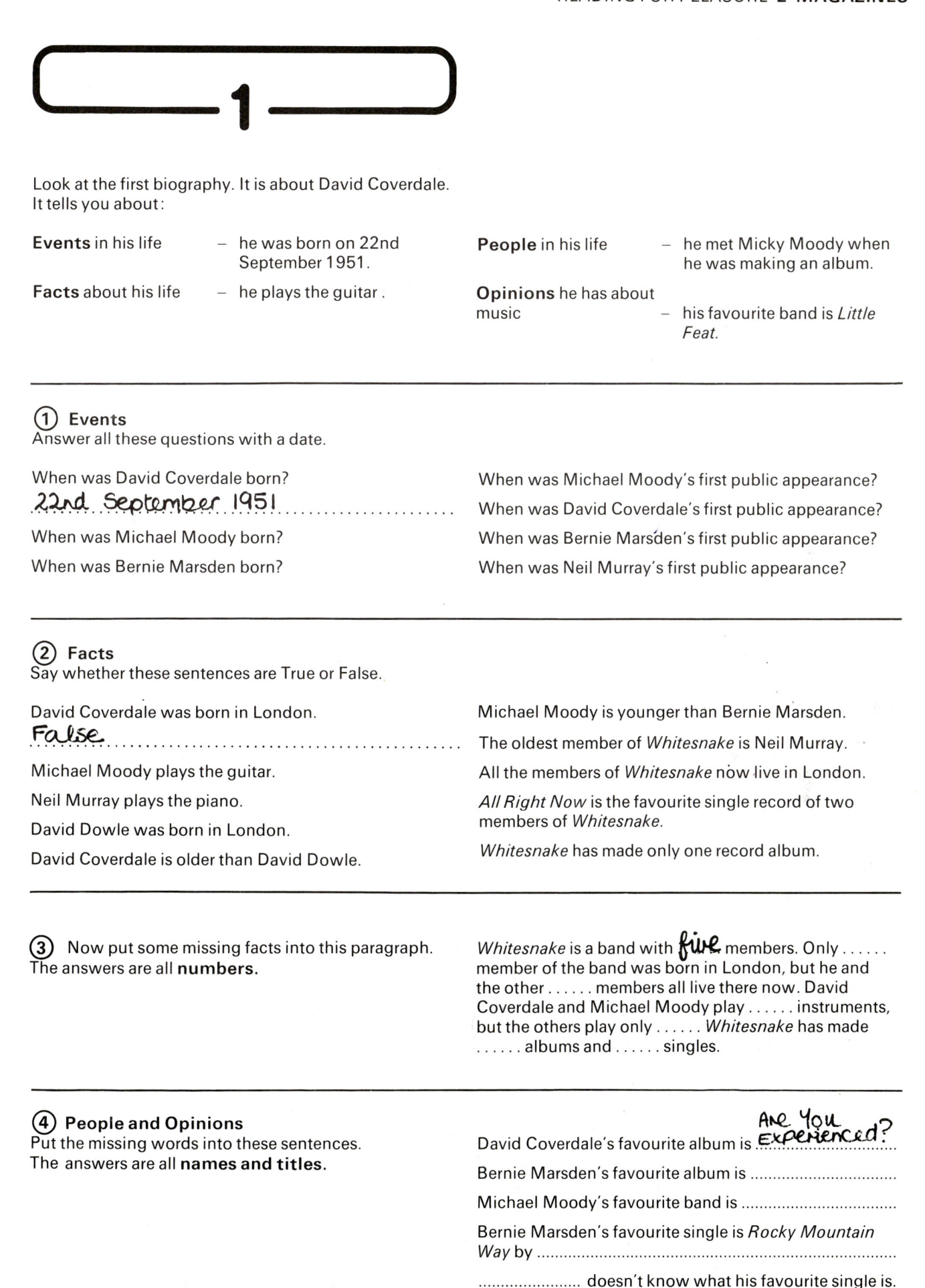

1

Look at the first biography. It is about David Coverdale.
It tells you about:

Events in his life — he was born on 22nd September 1951.

Facts about his life — he plays the guitar.

People in his life — he met Micky Moody when he was making an album.

Opinions he has about music — his favourite band is *Little Feat*.

---

① **Events**
Answer all these questions with a date.

When was David Coverdale born?
22nd September 1951

When was Michael Moody born?

When was Bernie Marsden born?

When was Michael Moody's first public appearance?

When was David Coverdale's first public appearance?

When was Bernie Marsden's first public appearance?

When was Neil Murray's first public appearance?

---

② **Facts**
Say whether these sentences are True or False.

David Coverdale was born in London.
False

Michael Moody plays the guitar.

Neil Murray plays the piano.

David Dowle was born in London.

David Coverdale is older than David Dowle.

Michael Moody is younger than Bernie Marsden.

The oldest member of *Whitesnake* is Neil Murray.

All the members of *Whitesnake* now live in London.

All Right Now is the favourite single record of two members of *Whitesnake*.

Whitesnake has made only one record album.

---

③ Now put some missing facts into this paragraph. The answers are all **numbers**.

Whitesnake is a band with *five* members. Only ...... member of the band was born in London, but he and the other ...... members all live there now. David Coverdale and Michael Moody play ...... instruments, but the others play only ...... *Whitesnake* has made ...... albums and ...... singles.

---

④ **People and Opinions**
Put the missing words into these sentences.
The answers are all **names and titles**.

David Coverdale's favourite album is *Are You Experienced?*

Bernie Marsden's favourite album is ....

Michael Moody's favourite band is ....

Bernie Marsden's favourite single is *Rocky Mountain Way* by ....

.... doesn't know what his favourite single is.

55

READING FOR PLEASURE 2 MAGAZINES

Read this biography of Elvis Presley carefully.

The King is dead: Long live the King!

The two-year-old Elvis, photographed with his parents, Gladys and Vernon Presley.

Elvis Presley was born on January 8th 1935, in Tulepo, Mississippi. His parents were poor, and they were very religious. They often took Elvis to church. That's where he first learned to sing. Most people feel that these religious songs had a big influence on Elvis' singing style.

Then, when he was a teenager, Elvis went to live in Memphis, Tennessee. He went to the local High School. He was an average student. The thing he was really interested in, was music.

One day, in 1955, he took his guitar to the Sun Recording Studio in Memphis. There he recorded two country 'n' western songs for his mother's birthday. One of them was called *That's all right Mama*. All her life she was very close to Elvis. The recording studio liked the songs and they liked the singer. His style was a mixture of two traditions, white country 'n' western, and blues – the music of the black people in the American South.

A few months later, Elvis met 'Colonel' Tom Parker. He took over Elvis' career. With his management, Elvis became popular not only in America, but all over the world. Soon, Elvis had his first smash hits – *Hound Dog, All Shook Up*, and many others. They were wonderful songs, sung by the greatest pop star in the history of pop music.

Some years later, Elvis was making Hollywood films like *Love Me Tender* and *King Creole*. He made many films – some people say too many. Some of them were not very good. But Elvis' fans were always loyal. They went to see all his films, and they bought all his records.

Elvis died aged 42. It was a sudden death. It came as a shock. Everyone knew Elvis was the king of rock 'n' roll. And everyone knows he will always be the king of rock 'n' roll. Long Live Elvis!

THE LAST TOUR

2

① Here are eight events in Elvis Presley's life but they are in the wrong order.
Can you put the events in the right order?

Elvis recorded 'That's all right Mama'.

Elvis died.

he made his first hit records

Elvis was born.

he learned to sing in church

Elvis met 'Colonel' Tom Parker.

Elvis went to school in Memphis.

he made Hollywood films

Now match each of the events listed above with one of these words and phrases about time, to make a paragraph about when the events happened. You will find words and phrases about time in the biography about Elvis. Use those words and phrases to help you.

In your paragraph, put these words at the **end** of their events:

suddenly   **in 1935**

and put these words and phrases at the **beginning** of their events:

one day   **then**   **soon**   **at first**

a few months later   **some years later**

② Here are some facts and opinions about Elvis. Can you find four facts and four opinions?

Elvis first recorded for Sun Studios.

They were wonderful songs.

Elvis' manager was 'Colonel' Tom Parker.

Elvis made many films.

Elvis made too many films.

Elvis went to live in Memphis.

Elvis will always be the king of rock 'n' roll.

The biggest influence on his singing style was religious music.

READING FOR PLEASURE **2 MAGAZINES**

3 Look at the first sentences in the biography.

> Elvis Presley was born on January 8th 1935, in Tulepo, Mississippi.
> His parents were poor and they were very religious.

'His' refers to Elvis Presley.　　'they' refers to his parents.

Here are some other people and events in Elvis' life:

They often took Elvis to church.	– Who were 'they'?	They went to see all his films.	– Who were 'they'?
She was very close to Elvis.	– Who was 'she'?	Some of them were not very good.	– What are 'them'?
He took over Elvis' career.	– Who was 'he'?	It came as a shock.	– What was 'it'?

3

Here is a paragraph about Elvis. But it does not make sense because the sentences are all in the wrong order.

Use your understanding of the facts, events, people and opinions in Elvis' biography to put the sentences in the right order. The notes at the side will help you:

NOTES

He helped Elvis' career enormously. First, he had talent. What were the reasons for his success? They will always remember him as the King. Second, he had a good manager. Elvis Presley was born in the 1930s. And third, Elvis has the most loyal fans in the world. Twenty years later, he was the world's most successful pop singer. It was a talent for combining the music of white people with the music of black people. Well, I can think of at least three.	1 Birth and childhood .... 2 Success .... 3 Reasons for success .... a .... Example: .... b .... Example: .... c .... Example: ....

skills check

You have read:　　**A magazine article** ...... about a pop group

　　　　　　　　　A biography　　　 ...... of a pop singer

You have practised:　**1 Reading about events.**

　　　dates and ages ...... born in 1951/died aged 42

　　　order　　　　 ...... first/second/then

　　　time　　　　　 ...... one day/soon/later

2 Reading about facts.

　　　numbers　　...... the band has five members/he recorded two songs

　　　places　　　...... born in Tulepo/lives in London

　　　information ...... he plays the drums/he made films

3 Recognizing words about people.

names and titles	Tom Parker	Gladys	Whitesnake
occupations	manager	mother	pop group
referring words	he	she	they

4 Recognizing opinions.

　　　...... they were wonderful/they were not very good

READING FOR PLEASURE 3 NON-FICTION

Reading for Pleasure
3. NON-FICTION

After they left the newspaper stand, Carl and Rosa bought a book called *This is London*.

They sat down in a London park to read it. They found it useful and interesting.

Here are parts of the book they were reading.

1 The COVER of the book. ▶

The TITLE
The AUTHOR

THIS IS LONDON
Philip Prowse

2 The INTRODUCTION to the book. ▼

Introduction

London is the biggest city in **1.**_____. More than seven million people live and work there.

London is also one of the most important cities in the **2.**____. It is a centre for business and for tourism.

In London, you can find some of the best theatres and **3.**_____ in the world. You can find old and new buildings, and many beautiful **4.**____.

This book begins with a little of London's **5.**____. Then we look at the London of today. You can see and do many things in London. We will have a look at this great **6.**__.

3 The CONTENTS of the book. ▼

Contents

		pages
1.	History of London	2–8
2.	Places to Visit	9–19
3.	Travelling in London	20–21
4.	Shopping	22–23
5.	London at Night	24–27
6.	Information and Advice	28–29

4 Some EXTRACTS from the book. ▼

Palaces

Buckingham Palace is the London home of the Queen. You can walk from Westminster Abbey to the Palace. The walk goes through St James's Park.

Churches

Westminster Abbey is one of the most famous churches in London. It is very near to the Houses of Parliament.

The Houses of Parliament

The Houses of Parliament are in Westminster. They are the centre of the British government. Members of Parliament (MPs) come from all over Britain. They meet in the Houses of Parliament.

Parks

Every visitor knows some of the parks of London. There are more than eighty of them! The best known parks near the centre of London are Hyde Park, Regent's Park and St James's Park.

Theatres and Cinemas

Most theatres and cinemas in London are in the *West End*. The nearest tube stations are Piccadilly and Leicester Square.

Shopping

Oxford Street is London's main shopping centre. Walk along Oxford Street from Marble Arch to Oxford Circus. You will pass hundreds of shops.

READING FOR PLEASURE 3 NON-FICTION

1

① Some words are missing from the Introduction. Read the whole text and then guess the missing words. There are some clues and an example to help you.

Clue 1:	One word for England, Scotland, Wales and N. Ireland.
Answer:	Britain

Clue 2:	Another word for the Earth.
Answer:	......
Clue 3:	Buildings where we keep old, historical things.
Answer:	......
Clue 4:	Open spaces, where we can walk or play.
Answer:	......
Clue 5:	Another word for the past.
Answer:	......
Clue 6:	Bigger than a town.
Answer:	......

② Below are some more extracts from the book. Guess which chapter you will find them in. You will need to look at the Contents list.

Example:
'On Saturday 2nd September 1666, there was a big fire.'
Answer: Chapter 1. History of London.

In which chapter will you find these:

'In 1066, William the Conqueror came to England.'

'You can buy anything from Harrods – from a pin to an elephant.'

'Perhaps you will visit London one day. Here is some advice.'

'The 'tube' is London's underground railway. The tube is quick and easy.'

'You can visit many interesting places in London. This chapter tells you about some of them.'

③ This is what Carl and Rosa said as they were reading the book. But some of the words are missing.

Use the extracts to help you to guess the missing words.
Six words are on page 58, and six are not.
The first two words are done for you.

Carl I'd love to see Buckingham Palace.

Rosa Yes, perhaps we can meet the Queen.
(**Queen** – from 'Palaces')

Carl She may not be at home.
(**home** – a guess!)

But we are quite near the Houses of Parliament in ......

Rosa Mm. I'm not very interested in politics. It sounds ......

Carl Oh no it isn't, Rosa. It's really very old and interesting there.

Rosa Well, maybe. But I do want to see Westminster Abbey.

Carl Mm. I don't like ...... very much.

Rosa Well it's not ...... from the Houses of Parliament. We can see them both at the same time.

Carl You're right. We can see them both tomorrow morning.

Rosa And then in the ...... we'll go to a park. It says here that there are over ...... of them in London!

Carl And I want to go shopping too! It says Oxford Street is good.

Rosa Good idea. But I need some money. I must go to the ...... tomorrow.

Carl Me too. But what about tonight, Rosa? I'd love to see a play. There are lots of ...... in London.

Rosa Oh I forgot! My friend Linda has got some ...... for a play tonight. Would you like to come with us, Carl?

Carl I'd love to! Thanks Rosa. What's the ...... of the play?

Rosa I don't know! Linda didn't say. Never mind – we can guess.

59

READING FOR PLEASURE 3 NON-FICTION

2

Here is a whole page from *This Is London*. Read it once quite quickly. Then look at the questions below.

Then read the text more carefully to choose the best answers.

4. Shopping

Oxford Street is London's main shopping centre. Walk along Oxford Street from Marble Arch to Oxford Circus. You will pass hundreds of shops.

You can buy clothes, shoes and toys in the larger stores: *Selfridges, John Lewis, Debenhams*. Or you can shop in the small boutiques.

People from all over the world shop in Oxford Street. Look at the crowds in the photograph on page one. How many of these people are English?

The best-known London store is not in Oxford Street. It is *Harrods* in *Knightsbridge*. You can buy anything in Harrods — from a pin to an elephant!

There are also hundreds of open-air markets in London. They sell all kinds of things: vegetables, clothes, records, furniture. The two best known markets are in Petticoat Lane and in Portobello Road.

Petticoat Lane is on the east side of London, near Liverpool Street station. The market is open on Sundays. You can buy anything there. Some of the things are very cheap. But not many things are both good and cheap!

Portobello Road market is in west London. You can get there by tube. The nearest tube stations are Notting Hill Gate and Ladbroke Grove. The market is very busy on Saturday. You will find old furniture and antiques on many of the stalls in Portobello Road.

Opposite: A busy market day in London's Portobello Road.

Choose the best answers.

THE TEXT	THE ILLUSTRATION
Selfridges is a a department store b a toy shop c a small boutique	The picture shows a a large department store b a street market c a main shopping centre
Harrods is a old b famous c expensive	The people are a tourists b Londoners c tourists and Londoners
To find an elephant in Harrods is a probable b possible c impossible	Portobello Road is a a busy tube station b a main shopping centre c an open-air market
Petticoat Lane market is open a every day of the week b only on Sundays c at the weekends	The things for sale are a antiques b vegetables c furniture

READING FOR PLEASURE **3** NON-FICTION

3

1 When you are reading a book or magazine about the subject 'Entertainment', you can **predict** some of the words you will read.

Example:

You probably **will** read these words ...... theatres / cinemas / sport

You possibly **won't** read this word ...... kitchen

Now look at the lists of words below, and for each one choose four words you probably will read, and one you possibly won't:

1 In a magazine about the theatre.	2 In a newspaper about sport.	3 In a film magazine.	4 In a description of a restaurant.	5 In a book about dancing.
stage actor performance score audience	winner loser actress race athletics	cinema waiter actor producer director	tasty sweet delicious tiring expensive	to move to step to jump to turn to travel

6 In a travel brochure.	7 In a guide to a large park.	8 In a book about driving.	9 In a comic about two young people.	
tickets grass prices fares planes	lake path trees seat petrol	quickly dangerously slowly passionately safely	to meet to like to kiss to love to clap	

2 Look at the words you said you would not find, and put them in the list where you would expect to find them.

skills check

You have read: **Parts of a book about London......**

the cover
the contents page
the introduction
an illustration
an extract from one chapter

You have practised:

1 Using clues to guess words ......

Clue	Answer
'another word for the past'	history

2 Using other sentences to guess words ......

'I need some money. I must go to the ......'

3 Using other words to guess meaning ......

'You can buy anything at Harrods'.   'Harrods' must be a shop.

4 Putting words into subject groups ......

Words		Subject
ticket/fare/plane	=	travel
win/lose/race	=	sport

5 Answering multiple choice questions ......

This is London is a a comic
 b a book ✓
 c a magazine

READING FOR PLEASURE 4 FICTION

Reading for Pleasure
4. FICTION

On their way to the theatre, Carl and Rosa went to a bookshop to buy a book each to read at home. Carl bought a book called *The House on the Hill*.

Before reading parts of Carl's book, look at the cover

and at the first illustration.

Now answer this question:

What do you think the book will be about?

a crime

b science-fiction

c love

d horror

e war

Now read Chapter One.

PART 1

It was a beautiful summer evening. Paul was happy. No more exams. College was finished. Now he needed a job. He wanted to be a writer and work for a newspaper. But first he needed a rest.

It was hot in the house. There was no wind.

'I'll go for a walk,' said Paul to himself. 'I'll go down to the river.'

Paul lived in a small town and he was soon outside in the country. He walked near the river and watched the water birds.

Suddenly, he saw the girl. She was standing alone, looking into the water. She was young, and very beautiful. She had long, dark hair, and she was wearing a pretty white dress.

Paul went up to her.

'Hello,' he said. 'What's your name?'

'I'm Maria,' she said, and she smiled at him.

Paul and Maria talked for a long time. The sun went down. It was nearly dark.

'I must go home,' said Maria.

'Where do you live?' asked Paul.

'In the big white house on the hill,' said Maria. 'Where do you live?'

'In the little brown house near the market,' said Paul.

They laughed. But Paul was sad. The house on the hill was big and important. Maria was rich, and he was poor. And Paul was in love.

1

READING FOR PLEASURE 4 FICTION

1

1 The Characters
The boy
a his name .... Paul
b wants to be ....
c money: rich / poor? ....
d feelings: happy /sad?
   at the beginning ....
   at the end ....
   about the girl ....

The girl
a her name .... Maria
b her age ....
c her money ....
d appearance ....
   her hair ....
   her dress ....

① *The House on the Hill* is a love story. Read the first page again, and **while** you are reading, make NOTES. Write one word only, like this:

2 The Place
a Paul walks. Where? .... river
b Paul lives. Where? ....
   town / city / country ....
c His house: size / colour? ....
d Her house: size / colour? ....

3 The Time
a Time of year .... Summer
b Time of day
   at the beginning ....
   at the end ....
c They talk: How long? ....

After you have finished reading, do not look back at the story, but use your notes to write about the boy / the girl / the place / the time.

② Here is another extract from the book. ▶

Before you read this part, you need to know:

Paul lives alone with his mother, a poor, kind woman.
Maria lives alone with her mother, a rich, ugly woman.
In this extract, Paul visits Maria's mother for the first time.

While you are reading the extract, think about:

Maria's mother – her feelings about Paul.
Maria – her feelings about Paul.
Paul – his feelings about Maria and her mother.
Money.

> 'So you want to marry my daughter?' The old woman said. Her voice was hard.
> Paul looked at her bravely. 'Yes,' he said. 'I love Maria and I want to marry her.'
> The old woman laughed.
> 'You! A poor student! No money, no father, nothing! My daughter will never marry you.'
> Paul said nothing. He looked at Maria. She did not look at him.
> 'I am poor now,' he said. 'But one day I'll be a famous writer.'
> The old woman laughed again. 'No,' she said. 'My daughter is not for you. She is going to be married soon. You will never see her again.'

After you have read the extract, try to predict the end of the story.
Here are five endings. Do you think they are:

impossible / possible / probable / certain?

1 Maria kills her mother.
2 Paul kills Maria's mother.
3 Maria marries Paul.
4 Maria marries someone – but not Paul.
5 Paul marries someone – but not Maria.

READING FOR PLEASURE 4 FICTION

2

Rosa wanted to buy a famous short story called *The Verger.* There were two EDITIONS of the book in the shop. One was very difficult to read, but the other was shorter and easier. Rosa bought the simplified edition.

Here are extracts from both books.
Text A is easier than Text B.

Before you read you need to know:

The Verger is about a man called Albert Foreman. He works in a church. But Albert cannot read or write. He loses his job cleaning the church. Then Albert opens a shop, selling cigarettes and he becomes rich and successful. Now Albert doesn't want to read!

While you are reading try to understand all of Text A, but do not try to understand all of Text B. Both texts describe Albert's success after he left the job in the church.

After you have read the extracts do the exercises on the next page – they are easy!

The Verger

TEXT A   SIMPLIFIED VERSION ▶

Title: The Verger
Author: Surname : Maugham
          Other(s) : W. Somerset

At the end of the month, Albert Foreman left St Peter's for ever. He opened a shop and sold cigarettes.
  Many people came into his shop because it was the only one in the street. He began to sell other things. But they were all things for smokers. He sold tobacco for pipes. He sold cigars and matches. And every week the shop became busier.

  *

  After a year, Albert's shop was making a lot of money. Then Albert had another idea.
  'Why don't we open another shop?' he said to his wife. His wife agreed with him.
  Albert Foreman walked round London. At last he found a long, busy street with no cigarette shop. Albert opened another shop in that street. A young man worked in the shop for him. The shop soon became very busy.
  Albert did the same thing again and again. After ten years, he owned ten cigarette shops. All of them were very busy and every week Albert put more and more money into the bank.

He considered the matter from every point of view and next day he went along the street and by good luck found a little shop to let that looked as though it would exactly suit him. Twenty-four hours later he had taken it and when a month after that he left St. Peter's, Neville Square, for ever, Albert Edward Foreman set up in business as a tobacconist and newsagent. His wife said it was a dreadful come-down after being verger of St. Peter's, but he answered that you had to move with the times, the church wasn't what it was, and 'enceforward he was going to render unto Cæsar what was Cæsar's. Albert Edward did very well. He did so well that in a year or so it struck him that he might take a second shop and put a manager in. He looked for another long street that hadn't got a tobacconist in it and when he found it, and a shop to let, took it and stocked it. This was a success too. Then it occurred to him that if he could run two he could run half a dozen, so he began walking about London, and whenever he found a long street that had no tobacconist and a shop to let he took it. In the course of ten years he had acquired no less than ten shops and he was making money hand over fist. He went round to all of them himself every Monday, collected the week's takings and took them to the bank.

◀ TEXT B   ORIGINAL VERSION

Author: W. Somerset Maugham
Title: The Verger

READING FOR PLEASURE **4 FICTION**

3

① Making notes

Complete these notes about this part of the story:

Title.................Author.................Main Character.................

First job.................Next job.................

Albert sold.................Albert made lots of.................

In ten years, A. opened.................He became.................

② Comparing

The word 'bank' is in both texts.
It is in line 19 in Text A, and line 21 in Text B.

The word 'business' is in Text B, but not in Text A.

1 Look in both texts for the words below, and complete the chart:

WORDS	TEXT A	TEXT B
bank	Yes Line 19	Yes Line 21
business	No —	Yes Line 6
cigars		
London		
matches		
money		
month		
newsagent		
shop		
ten		
tobacco		
tobacconist		

2 Which words are in Text A only?

Which words are in Text B only?

Which words are in Text A **and** Text B?

3 Which text is longer?

Which text is easier?

③ Making a summary

Choose a book you have read recently and make a record of it like this:

AUTHOR .... TITLE ....

SUMMARY
Was it short / long? Was it easy / difficult?
What kind of book was it? fiction / non-fiction / subject
What was it about? Characters / place / time / events
Did you like it?

skills check

You have read: Extracts from two books ...... a love story.
...... a famous short story.

You have practised:
1 **Making predictions before you read** ...... from the cover / from an illustration
2 **Making notes while you are reading** ...... about characters / place / time
3 **Comparing texts after you have read** ...... Longer / shorter / easier / more difficult
4 **Summarizing a story** ...... **title** – 'What was it called?'
author – 'Who wrote it?'
subject – 'What was it about?'
events – 'What happened?'
opinion – 'Did you like it?'

READING FOR PLEASURE 5 A THEATRE VISIT

Reading for Pleasure
5. A THEATRE VISIT

Carl and Rosa met Linda and her friend Tom at the theatre. They were going to see a play called *The Mousetrap* by Agatha Christie.

Rosa introduced Carl to Linda and Tom. Then there was just time for a drink before the play started.

Linda and Tom went to order the drinks, and Carl and Rosa went to buy a PROGRAMME about the play.

Here are some extracts from the theatre programme for *The Mousetrap*.

① ... about the **play**. ▼

From The Guinness Book of Records 1977

The longest continuous run of any show in the world is The Mousetrap by Dame Agatha Mary Clarissa Christie, D.B.E. (nee Miller, now Lady Mallowan) (b. Torquay, Devon, 15 Sept, 1890). This thriller opened on 25 Nov, 1952, at the Ambassadors Theatre (capacity 453) and moved after 8,862 performances 'down the road' to St. Martin's Theatre on 25 Mar, 1974. Its 9,478th performance on 21 Aug, 1975 surpasses even the former composite record of The Drunkard in Los Angeles, which ran from 1932–1953, and was revived as a musical.

② ... about the **theatre**. ▼

ST MARTIN'S THEATRE

The Theatre opened on 23rd November 1916 with a "comedy with music" called *Houp La!* which starred Gertie Millar and George Graves, under the management of C. B. Cochran who was also lessee of the Theatre. This was replaced after one hundred and eight performances by a very different type of entertainment in *Damaged Goods*—the first public performances in this country of the play.

③ ... about the **author**. ▼

THE MOUSETRAP and AGATHA CHRISTIE

It would be easy to write a statistical biography of Agatha Christie. She wrote fourteen plays; her eightieth book was published on her eightieth birthday in September 1970; more than three hundred and fifty million of her books have been sold in virtually every country in the world. In fact, in March 1962, UNESCO announced that Agatha Christie was the most widely read British writer in the world, with Shakespeare coming a poor second.

④ ... about the **actors**. ▼

THE MOUSETRAP
by
AGATHA CHRISTIE

Characters in order of their appearance

Mollie Ralston	PETRONELLA FORD
Giles Ralston	PETER PENRY-JONES
Christopher Wren	KEITH MORRIS
Mrs Boyle	MARGO CUNNINGHAM
Major Metcalf	DENNIS CHINNERY
Miss Casewell	WENDY MURRAY
Mr Paravicini	ROY HEPWORTH
Detective Sergeant Trotter	DAVID McALISTER

DENNIS CHINNERY

⑤ ... about what to do **after the show**. ▼

LUNCH · DINNER · SUPPER
FULL SERVICE 7 DAYS A WEEK

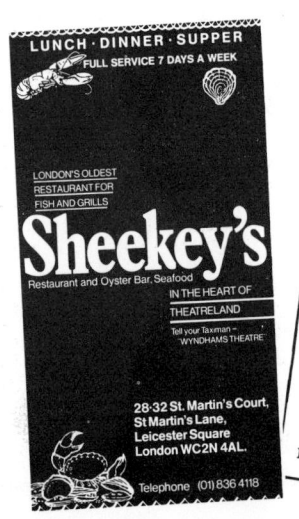

LONDON'S OLDEST RESTAURANT FOR FISH AND GRILLS

Sheekey's
Restaurant and Oyster Bar. Seafood
IN THE HEART OF THEATRELAND
Tell your Taxman—WYNDHAMS THEATRE

28-32 St. Martin's Court,
St Martin's Lane,
Leicester Square
London WC2N 4AL.
Telephone (01) 836 4118

After the theatre a Swiss snack is just the ticket.

After the curtain comes down you'll find some wonderful Swiss dishes being served right up to 1.00 a.m. (last orders midnight). Just because we open late we don't alter our programme.

Swiss Centre Restaurants, Leicester Square
In the heart of theatreland. 01-734 1291.

READING FOR PLEASURE 5 A THEATRE VISIT

1

① ...... about the play.
Answer **Yes** or **No**.

Is *The Mousetrap* a comedy?
Was *The Mousetrap* on in 1950?
Has *The Mousetrap* always been on in the same theatre?
Did *The Mousetrap* open in the spring?
Has *The Mousetrap* been on for more than 25 years?

② ...... about the theatre.
Answer **True** or **False**.

The St Martin's Theatre opened in the 1920s.
The first show at the St Martin's was *Houp La!*
Houp La! had less than 100 performances.
The first manager of the St Martin's Theatre was G. B. Cochran.
Damaged Goods was a musical comedy.

③ ...... about the author.
Fill in the blanks. You need four numbers and one name.

Agatha Christie was born in ...... She wrote ...... plays. By the time she was eighty, she had published ...... books, and more than ...... million of them have been sold. It has been said that more people read Agatha Christie than ...... !

④ ...... about the actors.
Give the right information:

How many characters are there in *The Mousetrap*?
Which character is the actor Keith Morris playing?
Which character is David McAlister playing?
Who is playing the part of Detective Sergeant Trotter?
Who is playing the part of Major Metcalf?

⑤ ...... about after the show.
Choose the best answers.

| 1 The Swiss Centre is |
| a a bar |
| b a restaurant |
| c a theatre |

| 2 You can order a meal at the Swiss Centre |
| a after midnight |
| b up to midnight |
| c up to 1.00 a.m. |

| 3 Sheekey's is open |
| a everyday |
| b weekdays |
| c weekends |

| 4 Sheekey's is near |
| a St Martin's Theatre |
| b Wyndham's Theatre |
| c Leicester Square |

| 5 The Swiss Centre and Sheekey's both advertise |
| a Swiss food |
| b sea food |
| c supper |

2

After the play, Carl, Rosa, Linda and Tom went to a restaurant near the theatre. They had all enjoyed *The Mousetrap* very much, and talked about it while they read the menu.

Then Linda told them she had four tickets for another play, *Julius Caesar* by William Shakespeare. The play was at the theatre in Stratford, and Linda offered to drive Carl, Rosa and Tom there on Saturday to see the town and the play.

While Carl and Rosa were thanking Linda, the waiter arrived. Rosa said she definitely didn't want a salad . . .

READING FOR PLEASURE 5 A THEATRE VISIT

Rosa, Carl, Linda and Tom enjoyed their visit to Stratford. On these two pages are some of the things they **said**. Use the things they **read** to complete the missing parts of the conversations.

① On the way. ▶

Carl   We're in Oxford.
       Is Stratford very far from here?

Tom   No, not very. Here's a map.

Carl   Thanks. Oh, it's only about . . . . . . kilometres.

② In Stratford. ▼

Rosa   I'd like to see Shakespeare's birthplace. Where is it?

Linda It's in . . . . . .

The Shakespearian Properties Stratford-upon-Avon

The following properties administered by the Shakespeare Birthplace Trust are open to visitors all the year round:

Shakespeare's Birthplace, Henley St
Anne Hathaway's Cottage, Shottery
New Place, Chapel Street
Hall's Croft, Old Town
Mary Arden's House, Wilmcote

For a descriptive leaflet please send stamped addressed envelope to the Director, The Shakespeare Centre, Stratford-upon-Avon.

TOWN GUIDE

③ In Shakespeare's birthplace. ▶

Linda I didn't know Shakespeare had any children.

Tom   I knew he had one, but I didn't know he had . . . . . .

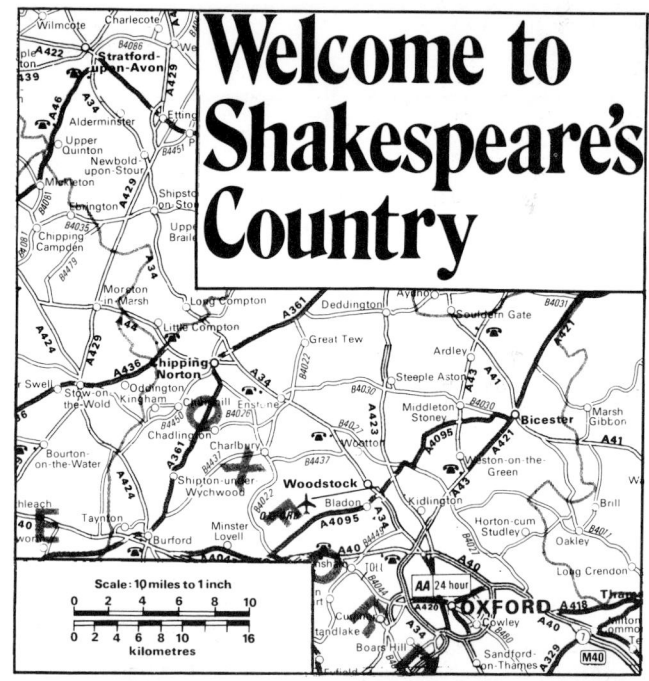

Welcome to Shakespeare's Country

A SHORT BIOGRAPHY
SOME IMPORTANT DATES

1556	Birth of Anne, daughter of Richard Hathaway.
1558	Elizabeth I became Queen of England.
1564	Birth of William Shakespeare, April 26th.
1582	Shakespeare married Anne Hathaway.
1583	Shakespeare's daughter, Susanna, born.
1585	Birth of Hamnet and Judith, Shakespeare's twins.
1592	Shakespeare already a player and a writer.
1599	Opening of Globe Theatre, Bankside.
1610	Shakespeare retired to New Place, Stratford.
1616	Death of Shakespeare, April 23rd.
1623	John Heminge and Henry Condell publish the first collected edition of Shakespeare's plays.

READING FOR PLEASURE 5 A THEATRE VISIT

④ In a bookshop. ▼

Tom *Julius Caesar* is about ancient Rome, isn't it?

Carl Yes, but it isn't a history play. It's like *Hamlet*, one of the . . . . . .

TABLE OF SHAKESPEARE'S PLAYS

PERIOD		COMEDIES	HISTORIES	TRAGEDIES
I	1584	Comedy of Errors Taming of the Shrew Two Gentlemen of Verona	1, 2, 3 Henry VI Richard III King John	Titus Andronicus
	1592			
	1594	Love's Labour's Lost	Venus and Adonis } poems Rape of Lucrece	
II		Midsummer-Night's Dream Merchant of Venice Merry Wives of Windsor Much Ado About Nothing As You Like It	Richard II 1 Henry IV 2 Henry IV Henry V	Romeo and Juliet
	1599			
III		Twelfth Night Troilus and Cressida Measure for Measure All's Well		Julius Cæsar Hamlet Othello Timon of Athens Lear Macbeth Antony and Cleopatra Coriolanus
	1608			
IV		Pericles Cymbeline Winter's Tale Tempest		
	1613		Henry VIII	

PART OF THE TEXT

ACT THREE
SCENE ONE

A crowd of people; among them ARTEMIDORUS *and the* SOOTHSAYER. *Flourish. Enter* CÆSAR, BRUTUS, CASSIUS, CASCA, DECIUS, METELLUS, TREBONIUS, CINNA, ANTONY, LEPIDUS, POPILIUS, PUBLIUS, *and others*

CÆSAR: The ides of March are come.
SOOTHSAYER: Ay Cæsar, but not gone.
ARTEMIDORUS: Hail Cæsar. Read this schedule.
DECIUS: Trebonius doth desire you to o'er-read
　At your best leisure this his humble suit.
ARTEMIDORUS: O Cæsar, read mine first; for mine's a suit
　That touches Cæsar nearer. Read it great Cæsar.
CÆSAR: What touches us ourself shall be last served.
ARTEMIDORUS: Delay not Cæsar, read it instantly.
CÆSAR: What, is the fellow mad?
PUBLIUS: 　　　　　　Sirrah, give place.　　　　10
CASSIUS: What, urge you your petitions in the street?
　Come to the Capitol.

CÆSAR *and the rest enter the Senate*

⑤ In the theatre.

Rosa And then this man Artemidorus wants Caesar to . . . . . . something. But Caesar says no!

Carl Thanks. The lights are going out – It's starting!

skills check

You have read:　Extracts from . . . . . . a theatre programme.
　　　　　　　　　　　　　　. . . . . . a road map.
　　　　　　　　　　　　　　. . . . . . a guide book.
　　　　　　　　　　　　　　. . . . . . a table.
　　　　　　　　　　　　　　. . . . . . a play.

You have practised:　**1 Reading for information** . . . . . . 'Is Stratford far from Oxford?'
　　　　　　　　　　　　　　　　　　　　　　　'No, here's a map.'

　　　　　　　　　　2 Reading for meaning . . . . . . *Characters in order of their appearance*
　　　　　　　　　　　　　　　　　　　　　　　Metcalf . . . . . . DENNIS CHINNERY

　　　　　　　　　　3 Reading for pleasure . . . . . . ARTEMIDORUS: Delay not Cæsar, read it
　　　　　　　　　　　　　　　　　　　　　　　CÆSAR: What, is the fellow mad?

READING REVISION 3

READING REVISION 3

REASONS for Reading 1 – What people read.

Study these pictures of people and the different magazines they read. Think about the people, about their lives and their interests. Then use the pictures to help you to complete the exercises on the next page.

1 *PLAYHOUR*

2 *JUDY*

3 *COUNTRY LIFE*

READING REVISION 3

4 *AMATEUR PHOTOGRAPHER*

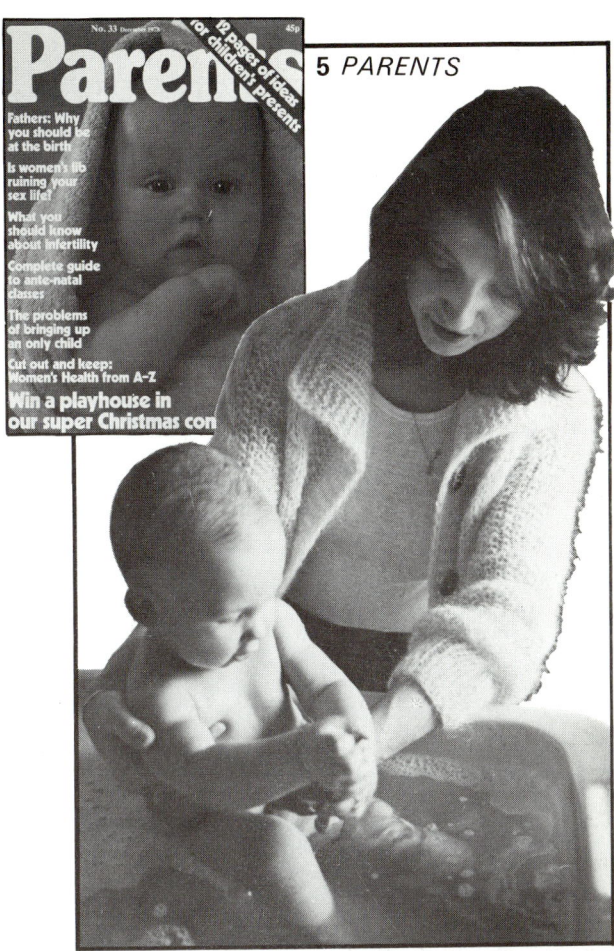

5 *PARENTS*

① Read this paragraph about *Playhour* and its readers.
Then look at the missing words and their meanings.

1 *Playhour* is usually bought by adults for children. It is a comic for both ...▼... and girls. Many children start reading *Playhour* from the age of five. Many of them read it for three or four years, up to the age of ...▼... or nine. Most *Playhour* readers live in large ...▲... like London or Liverpool, but the comic is enjoyed all over the country. *Playhour* is read by children from every ...▼... group.	The missing words are connected with: – *Playhour* is read by ⟨boys⟩ and girls. **sex** – *Playhour's* readers are aged three to ⟨eight⟩ or nine. **age group** – Many of *Playhour's* readers live in ⟨cities⟩. **home** – *Playhour* is not expensive and its readers are in every ⟨income⟩ group. **income**

② Now guess the missing words from these four paragraphs.

2 *Judy* is for ...... Most of them are ...... They live in all ...... of the country. Girls from all income groups read *Judy*, but the cheap price indicates that this magazine is probably most popular with girls from below average ...... group families.	4 *Amateur Photographer* is read more by ...... than by women. They are from all age ......, but the magazine is most popular with readers in their twenties and thirties. Most people live in ...... and not rural areas. Because photography can be an expensive hobby, it is not surprising that many readers of *Amateur Photographer* are from average and ...... average income groups.
3 *Country Life* is read by men and .... This magazine is popular with most ...... groups, especially middle-aged people. As the title of the magazine suggests many of its readers live in ...... areas, but it is also read by people in urban areas who are interested in sport, art, architecture, music and the theatre. Many of *Country Life's* readers have above ...... incomes.	5 *Parents* is designed for both men and women, but it is more often read by mothers and wives than by fathers and ...... *Parents'* readers are of all ......, but it is read most by women who are expecting their first child. The magazine sells well in urban areas. It is read in ...... and cities all over England. It is bought by ...... income groups, but mostly by average and above income groups.

READING REVISION 3

REASONS for Reading 2 – Why people read.

This page contains BACKGROUND INFORMATION about some readers. Read it quickly but carefully.

Dave is twenty-two. He works in a modern electronics factory. He enjoys reading about his hobby in his spare time.

Jane is in her forties. She is a food packer. Her husband likes gardening books. Her children read about history and geography. But Jane likes more exciting books, although she doesn't get much time to read them.

Alix is thirteen. She goes to school in London. She has to study French and German. She likes these subjects but she finds them difficult.

READING REVISION 3

Sam is over seventy. When he was a train driver, he saw a lot of small towns and villages. Now he is not working and has time to study their history.

Brenda and Max are students at a Technical College. Brenda is studying fashion design. Max is studying English – but he wants to be a pop musician.

Use the background information and the chart below to help you to do the exercises as quickly as you can.

WHO (readers)	WHAT (text types)	WHY (reasons for reading)	WHEN (time)	WHERE (place)
Jane	Science-fiction stories. Magazines and comics	Pleasure. Excitement. Escape to another world.	Any time she can find.	Travelling to work. At home.
Dave	Anything about the history of clocks.	Relaxation. Interest.	Evenings. Weekends.	At home. Library. Museum.
Alix	Non-fiction books about France and Germany – especially dictionaries.	Information. Help with her schoolwork.	Days, evenings. Not weekends.	At home At school.
Sam	Old maps and guides about the countryside.	Information. Pleasure. To find new places.	Any time.	At home. Places he visits.
Brenda and Max	Fashion magazines. Pop music papers.	Interest. Enjoyment. New ideas. To find jobs!	Brenda – all the time. Max – when not studying.	At home. At college. In class!
And what about you?				

1 True or False?

1 Jane likes reading gardening books.
2 Dave reads about his hobby in the evenings and at weekends.
3 Alix uses dictionaries to help her with her schoolwork.
4 Sam only likes reading old maps at home.
5 Brenda and Max both like to read books connected with their studies.

2 Rearrange the words to make complete sentences.

1 doesn't – connected – his – with – job – books – Dave – read

2 all – Sam – parts – country – of – maps – visits – old – find – the – to

3 and – them- advertisements – with – Brenda – magazines – Max – and – in – read – job – papers

4 children – Jane's – like – husband – science-fiction and – don't – stories

5 non-fiction – lot – French – Alix – German – and – a – uses – books – about – of

READING REVISION 3

3 Choose the best answers.

1 a Max
   b Sam } has lots of time to read what he wants.
   c Dave

2 For her schoolwork, Alix must use

a recipes

b timetables

c dictionaries

3 Sam reads old maps because

a he's a historian

b he's a train driver

c he's interested in the history of the country

4 Jane reads science-fiction

a at work

b in her spare time

c at weekends only

5 Max reads pop music papers

a at college only

b at home only

c anywhere

4 Guess the missing words.

...... reads? All kinds of people! The old, the young, everyone. And ...... do people read? For a variety of reasons. Some for pleasure others because they have to. And ...... do people read? Well sometimes not often, but other people read all the time, day and night. And ......? The answer is simple – anywhere and everywhere. But the most important question is ...... do people read? Adverts? Stories? Science books? Maps? It could be anything! Ask your family and friends all these questions. Then make your own ...... of who reads what, why, when and where!

INDEX

Alphabetical index of text types and other special features in the book.

A-Z street atlas	6
abbreviations	
addresses	2, 6, 78
dates	2, 8
dictionary entry	33
directions	12
distances	12
height/length	2-5
international car registration	8
size	5
time	13
see also	
forms, handwriting, messages, notices, posters.	
advertisements	
food	44
jobs	20
travel	44
see also	
notices	
alphabetical index	23
see also index	
area map	7
article, magazine	54, 57
author	58, 64, 66
biography	
of pop group in magazine	54
of Elvis Presley	56
of Shakespeare	68
block capitals	26, 27
books	
fiction	62-65
non-fiction	58-61
brochure, hotel	44
bubble	50, 52
caption	50
cartoon	50, 53
chapter	62
chart	
personal information	4, 73
directions/distances	12
columns	21
comics	50, 53, 70, 73
contents	58
conversation	
(*throughout book*)	
phone conversations	30, 36
cover	58, 62
crossword puzzle	24
description	2
diagram	11
dialogue	
see also conversation	
diary	46
dictionary	
entry	33
foreign language	73
directions	
conversational	10
maps/charts	12
handwritten message	13
directories (phone)	23
extract	59, 63
fiction	62-65
form	
booking holidays	28
enrolment	26
International Student Travel	3
staff record card	2
survey	29
guides	
guide book: Barbados	44
hospital guide	21
town guide: Stratford	68
travel guide: accommodation	16
handwriting	
form	2, 26, 28
letter	3, 8, 40
memo/message/notes	13, 31, 32, 46
notices	34, 36
illustrations	44, 45, 60, 62
index	
alphabetical (names)	23
alphabetical (streets)	6, 7
cities on a map	9
international car registration	8
instructions	
directions (left, right, etc.)	11, 13
form filling	26-29
introduction	58
key	
area map	7
plan of British Library/Museum	13
timetable, British Rail	17
weather report, newspaper	9
letters	
of alphabet (*throughout book*)	
letter	3, 40, 41
list	20
love story	63
magazine	54-57
article	54
cartoon	53
fashion	73
opinion page	40
other	70, 71, 73
map	
area	7
grid	6, 8
old	73
road	68
Spain	8
street	6, 11
Switzerland	12
underground	14
memo	31
menu	42
message	
formal handwritten	31
informal handwritten	13, 46
on notice-board	34, 36
newspaper	
cartoon	53
pop music paper	73
weather forecast	9
non-fiction	58-61
notes	
informal, rapidly written	31
study skills	57, 65
notices/notice-board	
airport	21
enrolment notice-board	18, 19
student union notice-board	34-37
numbers	
(*throughout book*)	
painting	38
phone	
conversations	30, 36
directories	23
photograph	
(*throughout book*)	
passport photograph	3
portrait	38
pictures	38
picture stories	50-53
plan	
British Library/Museum	13
play	
'The Mousetrap'	66
'Julius Caesar'	69
portrait	38
posters	34-37
print	
large	35
small	35
prose (examples of)	
biography	54
fiction	62, 64
non-fiction	58, 60
a story (narrative)	46
see also some of the introductory texts	
puzzle	
anagrams	23
crossword	24
questionnaire	29
road map	68
rows	21
scale	
area map	7
map of Switzerland	12
road map	68
science-fiction	62, 73
short story	64
signs	11
signature	26
story	
fiction	62-65
love story	63
(narrative: a story in the book)	46
picture stories	50-53
short story	64
stories, general	73
strip cartoon	50, 51
symbols	
hotel accommodation	16
travel: British Rail	17
travel: London Underground	14
other	17
tables	
height/length	4
Shakespeare's plays	69
(substitution table)	39
telegram	33
telephone	
see also phone	
text	60, 64, 69
theatre programme	66
time	13, 21, 31
timetable	17
titles	
of books	58, 64, 65
of people: Mr/Ms, etc.	26
warning	
police poster	34

ACKNOWLEDGEMENTS

The authors are grateful to members of staff at Ealing College of Higher Education and The Pathway Centre who helped in the development of the materials, to Mike Esplen and Kate Melliss of Heinemann Educational Books and to those students who acted as photographic models—Fatiha Mills, Paul Grey and Kathleen Sinclair Perry.

While every effort has been made to trace the owners of copyright material in this book, there have been some cases where the publishers have been unable to find the sources. We should be grateful to hear from anyone who recognises their copyright material and who is unacknowledged. We shall be pleased to make the necessary corrections in future editions of the book.

The authors and publishers wish to thank the following for the use of their material and for providing illustrations:

Sidgwick and Jackson Ltd for permission to include the size guide from *Superwoman* by Shirley Conran. Published Sidgwick and Jackson Ltd, 1975, Penguin Books Ltd, 1977—**p.5.**
Geographer's A—Z Map Co Ltd and the Ordnance Survey for permission to include the street maps and indices from *London Street Atlas and Index*, based upon Ordnance Survey maps with the permission of the Controller of Her Majesty's Stationery Office. Crown Copyright—**pp. 6, 7, 11 and 22.**
The Controller of Her Majesty's Stationery Office and the Department of the Environment for the road signs from *The Highway Code* (Prepared by Department of Transport and C.O.I. Crown Copyright 1978)—**pp. 11, 17 and 22.**
The British Museum for permission to use the *Ground Floor Plan* and *Key* to The British Museum—**p. 13.**
London Transport for permission to reproduce the Underground Map and the symbols—**pp. 14, 15 and 17.**
British Railways Board for the extract from Paddington to Paignton passenger timetable—**p. 17.**
The Post Office for permission to use the *London Telephone Directories A—Z*, published 1978 and an extract from an entry in *L—R Directory*, 1978—**p. 23.**
Oxford University Press Ltd for permission to include the entry on 'message' from *The Oxford Advanced Learner's Dictionary of Current English* by A. S. Hornby (3rd ed. 1974) © Oxford University Press 1974—**p. 33.**
The Festival Office, Thames Polytechnic for permission to reproduce their Thames Film Festival poster (1977)—**p. 36.**
The Cardigan Hall Theatre, Richmond for permission to use the poster for *As You Like It*, performed by the Richmond Shakespeare Society, February 1978—**p. 36.**
Mr Tom Baker and The British Broadcasting Corporation for the photograph from *Dr Who: The Terror of the Zygons*. BBC Copyright Photograph—**p. 40.**
Thames Television for the photograph from *The Sweeney*—**p. 40.**
Sealink U.K. Ltd for the 'Sail Away' advertisement (1978)—**p. 44.**
Frank Cooper Ltd for the Frank Cooper 'Oxford' Marmalade advertisement—**p. 44.**
Susie Home for the photograph of Barbados—**p. 44.**
Tony Morris for illustrations—**pp. 46—47.**
Leslie Branton for illustrations—**pp. 50—51.**
Tiger magazine for extracts from 'Skid Solo' (*Tiger* 19.8.78) and 'Billy's Boots' (*Tiger* 19.8.78)—**p. 52.**
Polystyle Publications Ltd for the illustration from *Pippin in Playland* (Playland Holiday Summer Special 1978)—**p. 53.**
Marvel Comics Ltd for the illustration from *Star Wars* magazine No. 25 (26.7.78) © Marvel Comics Ltd 1979—**p. 53.**
D. C. Thomson & Co Ltd for the illustration from 'Bobby Dazzler', *Bunty—Judy Summer Special 1978* and the cover of *Judy* No. 993—**pp. 53 and 70.**
The Daily Mail for the cartoon by Don Roberts that appeared in Holiday Mail section, *The Daily Mail* 21.1.79—**p. 53.**
Rock On magazine for the Bandfile No. 4: Whitesnake from *Rock On* No. 4 August 1978,—**p. 54.**
The Cinema Bookshop for the photograph of Elvis Presley—**p. 56.** (centre).
Heinemann Educational Books Ltd and the author for permission to use extracts from *This is London* by Philip Prowse. Published in Heinemann Guided Readers Series 1977—**pp. 58, 59 and 60.**
Chris Gilbert for the photographs—**pp. 58 and 60.**
Heinemann Educational Books Ltd and the author for permission to use extracts from *The House on the Hill* by Elizabeth Laird. Published in Heinemann Guided Readers Series 1978—**pp. 62 and 63.**
Bill Heyes for the photograph—**p. 62.**
G. J. Galsworthy for the illustration—**p. 62.**
Heinemann Educational Books Ltd and the rewriter for permission to use extract from the retold version of *The Verger and Other Stories* by W. Somerset Maugham, retold by John Milne. Published in Heinemann Guided Readers Series 1975—**p. 64.**
Elizabeth Grant for the illustration—**p. 64.**
A. P. Watt Ltd for permission to reproduce the original version of text from *The Verger* by W. Somerset Maugham (*The Complete Short Stories of W. Somerset Maugham*, Vol III). Published by William Heinemann Ltd 1951—**p. 64.**
Guinness Superlatives Ltd for permission to include an extract from *The Guinness Book of Records*, published by Guinness Superlatives Ltd, 1977—**p. 66.**
Swiss Centre Restaurants for permission to reproduce their advertisement—**p. 66.**
Sheekey's Restaurant for permission to reproduce their advertisement—**p. 66.**
Peter Saunders for permission to include an extract from 'The Mousetrap and Agatha Christie' and the cast list for the play, *The Mousetrap* that appeared in the theatre programme—'The Mousetrap—St Martin's Theatre' (27th Year edition No. 39, December 1978)—**p. 66.**
Julia McDermot Ltd for permission to use the photograph of Dennis Chinnery—**p. 66.**
Martin Tickner of Theatreprint Ltd for permission to use an extract from his article on St Martin's Theatre that appeared in the theatre programme 'The Mousetrap—St Martin's Theatre' (27th Year edition No. 39, December 1978)—**p. 66.**
The Shakespeare Centre, Stratford-upon-Avon for permission to reproduce the list of properties administered by the Shakespeare Birthplace Trust—**p. 68.**
The Automobile Association for permission to reproduce the map on Shakespeare's Country—**p. 68.**
Mary Evans Picture Library for the print of William Shakespeare—**p. 68.**
The Heart of England Tourist Board for permission to reproduce material on Stratford-upon-Avon—**p. 68.**
William Collins Sons & Co Ltd for permission to reproduce the Table of Shakespeare's Works from *The Complete Works of William Shakespeare* (Tudor edition 1951) edited by Peter Alexander—**p. 68.**
The Royal Shakespeare Company for the photograph from the production of *Julius Caesar* at the Aldwych Theatre, London 1975, starring John Wood (Brutus) and Mark Dignam (Julius Caesar)—**p. 69.**
Henry Grant Photo Library for photograph no. 2—**p. 70.**
Simon Brown Photographers, Leamington Spa, for photograph no. 2—**p. 70.**
Colorsports for photograph no. 3—**p. 70.**
Country Life magazine for permission to use the cover of *Country Life* (7th December, 1978)—**p. 70.**
Playhour magazine for permission to use the cover of *Playhour* (20th January, 1979)—**p. 70.** *Playhour*, published every Wednesday by IPC Magazines Ltd.
THE MAGIC ROUNDABOUT © Serge Danot, licensed by BBC Enterprises.
The editor of *Amateur Photographer* magazine for his permission to use the cover of *Amateur Photographer* (8th December, 1978)—**p. 71.**
Parents magazine for permission to use the cover of *Parents* (No. 33, December 1978)—**p. 71.**
Hedgehog Design for photographs Nos. 4 and 5—**p. 71.**
Fontana Paperbacks for permission to use the cover of *The First Men in the Moon* by H. G. Wells (Fontana Science Fiction, Sixth Impression, January 1978)—**p. 72.**
Transworld Publishers Ltd for permission to use the cover of *The Chariot of the Gods* by Erich Von Daniken. Published by Corgi Books 1975—**p. 72.**
Model and Allied Publications Ltd for permission to use the cover of *Clocks* magazine (Vol. 1, No. 8, February 1979)—**p. 72.**
Heinemann Educational Books Ltd for permission to use the covers of *Get to Know Germany* by Ian MacDonald, 1975 and *Life in France* by H. F. Brookes and C. E. Fraenkel, 1976—**p. 72.**
George G. Harrap & Co Ltd for permission to use the cover of *Harrap's New Shorter French and English Dictionary* (Part Two—revised edition 1979)—**p. 72.**
Hedgehog Design for the photographs—**p. 72.**
R. H. Baynton-Williams for permission to use an extract from *Investing in Maps* by Roger Baynton-Williams, published Barrie and Rockliffe 1969, Corgi 1971—**p. 73.**
Conde Nast Publications Ltd for permission to use the cover of *Vogue* magazine (January 1979)—**p. 73.**
New Musical Express magazine for permission to use the cover of *New Musical Express* (9th December, 1978)—**p. 73.**
Hedgehog Design for the photographs—**p. 73.**

Contents

Preface
Mary's Story
My God is So Great
Jesus Heals
How Did You Spend Your Time?
God's Grace
His Precious Blood
God's Peace
Table of Love
Be Strong
No Greater Love
Bless The Lord

Preface

In 1966 I became a part of Fred and Arlene Davis' family from Camden. Arlene was a great pianist and singer for the Rockport Baptist church. The Davis's children sang and played instruments, and this exposure from my new extended family is where my love for music began. Arlene gave me piano lessons at that time and I was soon playing and rehearsing special music for church services. We often practiced after school and had fun. That year I began playing organ while she played piano at the church.

I have many fond memories of all the good times at the Davis home. I loved playing the old hymns. The first hymn I learned was "Wonderful Words Of Life". I feel it was a special gift from God to be able to play in church at such an early age. Soon I was playing organ one week and piano the next.

People started to approach me asking, "would you teach me?" After consideration I decided why not? So I started to teach others and felt such joy to see others learning and playing the piano.

Religious music is my favorite genre, the old Hymns are beautiful to sing and play. My favorite song is "Amazing Grace" because it reminds me of His Grace and how he came down from Heaven to save me from my sins and the promise of eternal life thereafter.

I have had other teachers who were also amazing musicians. All of my teachers taught me well. From them I learned classical, ragtime and blues. With this background, I sat down one day and wrote a melody, which led to chords, to lyrics and voila!, I had my first composition. This led to many other inspirational songs included in this book. It is a learning process and requires many hours. I am grateful to have had my friend and singer Connie Keep to interpret my compositions and bring them to musical life. My mother Mary Hodgkin's deserves credit for introducing me to the Holy Bible which she read to us kids all the time.

This book is my first endeavor and we enjoyed putting it together for you and hope you enjoy and are inspired by it, as I was inspired by dear and patient Arlene Davis.

In the future I am planning a children's book of songs.

Mary Taylor

Mary's Story

My interest in piano began before my teen years. I was influenced by listening and hearing Gospel songs played at our church. My first piano teacher was Arlene Davis who took me on as a student when I was 12 years old. After completing "Junior Hymn books 1 and 2 she had me playing four part harmony.

Another teacher I was blessed to have studied with was Glen Jenks, he taught me for three years, he loved to teach "rag time" music, his specialty.

I also studied under Carrie Landrith Clements, a very good pianist and Christian music player who passed a lot of her knowledge of Gospel songs to me. She taught me about theory and arrangement. She had many recitals, which were a lot of fun and helpful in my development.

Soon I began to play for the congregation at Rockport Baptist Church. It was a dream come true for me and I couldn't have done it without the support and inspiration from these fine musicians and God's gift to me as a pianist.

I love music and love inspiring others with my music. Several years ago I decided to write my own songs. I went to Bay Chamber Of Music School, and there I found another outstanding teacher named Mary Ann Driscoll. She helped me with some of my earlier compositions

I hope you enjoy these songs I have written. I intend on continuing writing and playing. It's been an interesting journey and I feel so blessed to be doing what I love and sharing with others.

Sincerely,

Mary Taylor

My God Is So Great
Lead sheet

1. I see the heavens sunlight and feel the sun shining bright I see the moon in it's space and know how it was all placed My God is so great and I will praise his name My God is so great and shall be praised

2. I see the pow-r of God and see his greatness shine bright I see the stars in their space and know it is by God's grace My God is so great and shall be praised

Bridge
I see the glory of God and feel his amazing grace filling my soul with his great love

Final Refrain
My God is so great and

Psalms 95:3 For the Lord is a great God
Music Words Composed by Mary Taylor © 2020

| C | B♭/G | G^sus/C | F | B♭ |

I will praise his name   My God is so great and

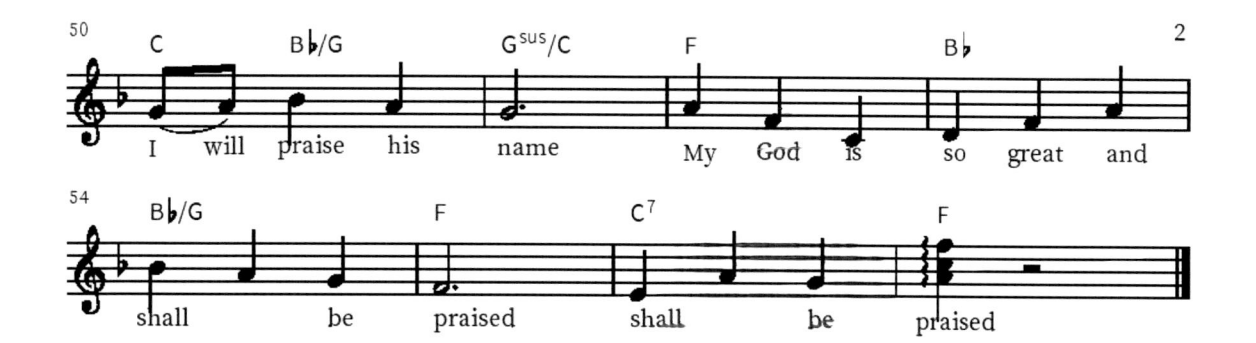

| B♭/G | F | C⁷ | F |

shall be praised   shall be praised

Jesus Heals
Lead Sheet

Refrain ♩=120

Je - sus heals the bro - ken heart - ed
He hears their cry in the dark night
gen - tly he says I will give you peace mer - cy and

1. Verses 1-2
2. Verses 3
grace mer - cy and grace

Fine Verses 1-3
1. Love joy peace
2. Grace bliss calm
3. Save Seek help

wor - ries and pain Rest
sor - rows and hurt Still
sad - nes and loss Hush

strength trust God will com - fort us
weak faith God will give us strength
my soul God is al - ways near

Psalms 34:18 The Lord is near to the broken hearted and saves those who are crushed in spirit. Music Words by Mary Taylor © 20203

How Did You Spend Your Time?
Lead Sheet

♩=108 Introduction | C | F C | G C | G C | C |

1. As I stand in the pres-ence of the Lord my hand shakes As I look up-on the kind-ness of his lov-ing face He takes me by the hand through the times of life I re-mem-ber all that He said

Chorus
How did you spend your time? Were you kind? (Were you kind?) Did you lend a help-ing hand? Did you walk with Je-sus? Did you tell a friend? Yes how did you spend your time?

2. He showed me the won-der-ful

Music Composed by Mary Taylor Words by Lillian Haynes © 2020

times of my life the good and the bad the hap-py the sad

When it was ov-er I saw a bright light there stood Je-sus

He had paid the price so I could go to hea-ven

for the rest of my life so what did you do with your life

Chorus

How did you spend your time? Were you kind (Were you kind)

Did you lend a help-ing hand? Did you walk with Je-sus?

Did you tell a friend? Yes how did you spend your time?

Music Composed by Mary Taylor Words by Lillian Haynes © 2020

God's Grace
Lead Sheet

Refrain

My grace is suf-fi-cient for you in weak-ness I will give you strength in the storms of life rest in my hand I will help you stand my grace is suf-fi-cient for you al-ways

1. I asked the Lord How do I go on my tri-als seem hard to bear I need you O God to-day help me be hum-ble as a child in your pres-ence I pray
2. I asked the Lord How can I go on my bur-dens seem hard to bear I trust you O God to-day help me have peace with-in my heart
3. I heard God say lean on me to-day when you have no strength to stand take my hand and trust in me I will give joy with-in your heart

2 Corinthians 12:9 And he said, My grace is sufficient for thee: for my strength is made perfect in weakness: Music Words by Mary Taylor © 2020

2.

34
Ab — Fm7 — Bb — Ab — Fm7 — Bb
I will seek you to-day have faith in me to-day

40 Refrain
Eb — Fm7 — Cm — Eb — Bb7 — Fm — Bb — Bb7
My grace is suf - fi - cient for you in weak-ness

44
Eb — Eb/G — Fm7 — Bb — Eb — Ab
I will give you strength in the storms of life rest in my hand

50
Bb — Ab — Bb — Eb
I will help you stand my grace is suf - fi - cient

54
Bb7 — Eb — Bb
for you al - ways my grace is

57
Eb — Fm7 — Bb7 — Eb
suf - fi - cient for you al - ways

His Precious Blood
Lead Sheet

♩=104

1. Je-sus came down from glo-ry to die for the lost
2. Je-sus came down from hea-ven to die on a cross

He paid the price for all our sin   Let us glo-
He bore our sins to set us free   Let us praise

ri-fy his name for-ev-er more   His prec-ious
and bless his name for-ev-er more

blood was shed for you and me   so we may live   to cleanse our

souls   (Bridge)   3. I saw his face and

found God's a-maz-ing grace   I bowed down at his feet his

mer-cy is com-plete   (Refrain) His prec-ious blood was shed for you and

---

1 Peter 1:19 It was the precious blood of Christ, as of a lamb without blemish and with out spot. Music Words Composed by Mary Taylor © 2020

| C7 | **1.** F | **2.** Gm | C | F |

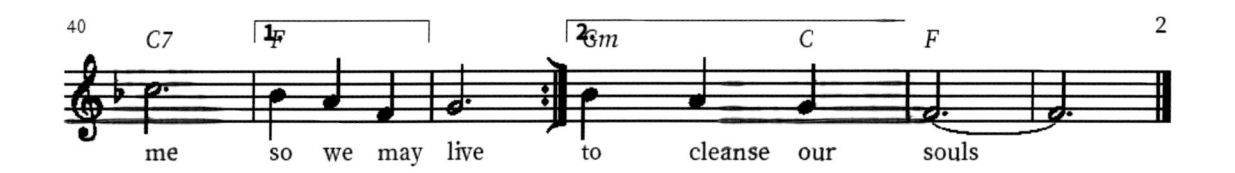

me   so we may live   to   cleanse our   souls

God's Peace
Lead Sheet

♩=114

There is a peace that comes from God a peace of hope for all who wait on the Lord He gives us hope and peace with-in our hearts

1. *There are dark clouds in the sky be-fore dawn a rain storm comes my way yet God is with me hearts*

2. *Deep in the night I can feel the love of God keep-ing me safe in his arms I do not fear hearts*

3. *When I feel lost God will help me find the way to live and trust*

Isaiah 40:31 But they that wait on the Lord shall renew their strength; Music Words Composed by Mary Taylor © 2020

Final Refrain

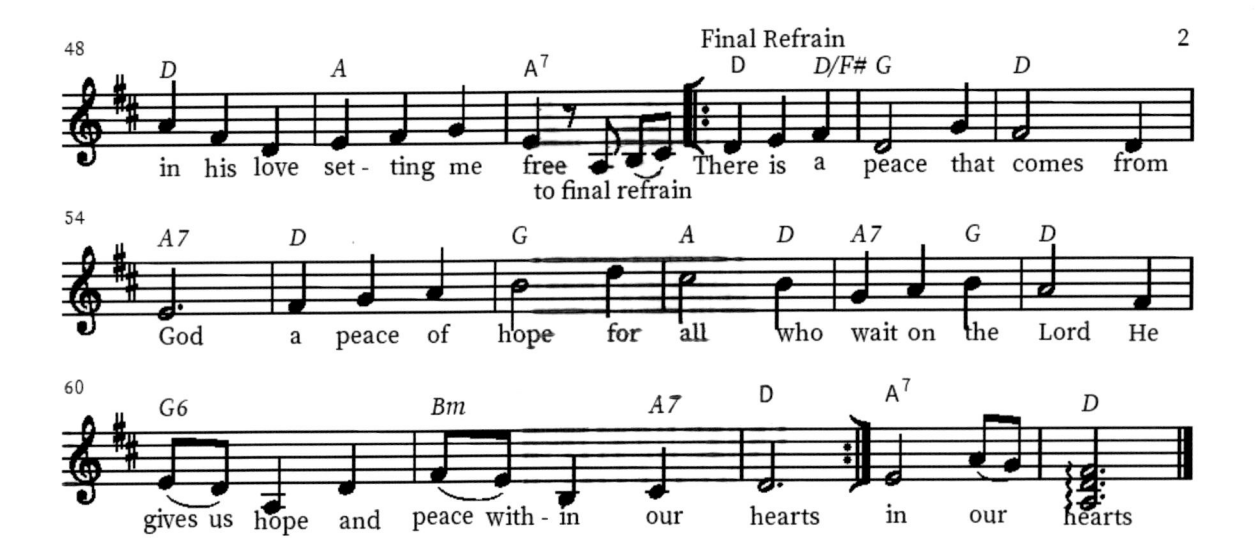

| D | A | A7 | D D/F# G | D |

in his love set-ting me free / to final refrain There is a peace that comes from

| A7 | D | G | A | D | A7 | G | D |

God a peace of hope for all who wait on the Lord He

| G6 | Bm | A7 | D | A7 | D |

gives us hope and peace with-in our hearts in our hearts

Table Of Love
Lead Sheet

♩=104

Refrain
Come to the ta-ble of love Come lift up his ho-ly name
Come take this bread and wine in re-mem-brance of him
1. Je-sus spoke these words of love I give you life
2. Je-sus spoke on the last day I give you life these
and for-give all your sins be-lieve in me spir-it and
words I speak to you to-day are
grace Come to the tab-le of love Come lift up his ho-ly name
Come take this bread and wine in re-mem-brance of
him 3. Lord I pray draw us close to you to-day

John 6:35 "I am the bread of life" Music
words Composed by Mary Taylor © 2020

Hold us close with in your lov- ing mer- cy and grace

Refrain
Come to the ta- ble of love Come lift up his ho- ly name Come take this bread and wine in re- mem- brance of him Come to the ta- ble of love

Be Strong
Lead Sheet

♩=120

Refrain
Be strong and cou-ra-geous do not be a-fraid for the Lord will nev-er for-sake you.

1. Rain comes down my clouds brok-en heart filled with pain winds may blow and I feel a-lone I will rest in the Lord God is with me
2. Storms brings fear be-come dark sor-row and strife trials may come but I will find peace in as the Lord for I know God is with me
3. Tears come down God will re-move be-cause he cares joy and love my soul set free as the sun shines I know God is with me

Psalms 31:24 Be strong and courageous Music
Words Composed by Mary Taylor © 2023

No Greater Love
Lead Sheet

1. God sent his son to die for our sins His blood was shed to wash a-way sin
2. God gave his son to die for the lost to set them free for e-ter-nal-ly
3. God sent Jesus to earth down be-low to save the world so that they may live

Refrain:
There's no love great-er than God's true love
There's no love great-er than to lay his life for his friends
lay his life for his friends lay his life for his friends

4. Be-lieve God's word re-cieve him to-day He is the truth and he is the way

to final refrain

Final Refrain:
There's no love

Music Words Composed by Mary Taylor © 2020

Music Words Composed by Mary Taylor © 2020

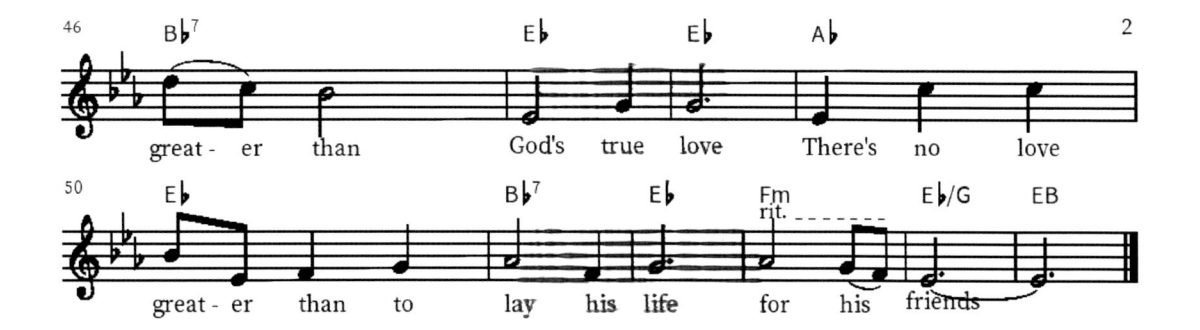

Bless The Lord
Lead Sheet

♩=112

Introduction

1. Wor - ship the
2. Wor - ship the
3. Come to -

Lord to - day Come praise his name Come and see
king to - day Come bless his name Come and know
day and re - joice Come give him thanks Come lift up

the love of God so rich and free Bless the Lord
the mer - cy of the Lord so true
your voic - ices and praise his name

Bless his name for he is good Bless the Lord Bless his name

1. for - ev - er more
2. for - ev - er more to bridge

Bridge

for - ev - er more to final refrain

Final Refrain

Bless the Lord Bless his name for he is good Bless the Lord

Psalms 145:2 Every day will I bless thee; and I will praise your name forever and ever Music Words Composed by Mary Taylor © 2020

41

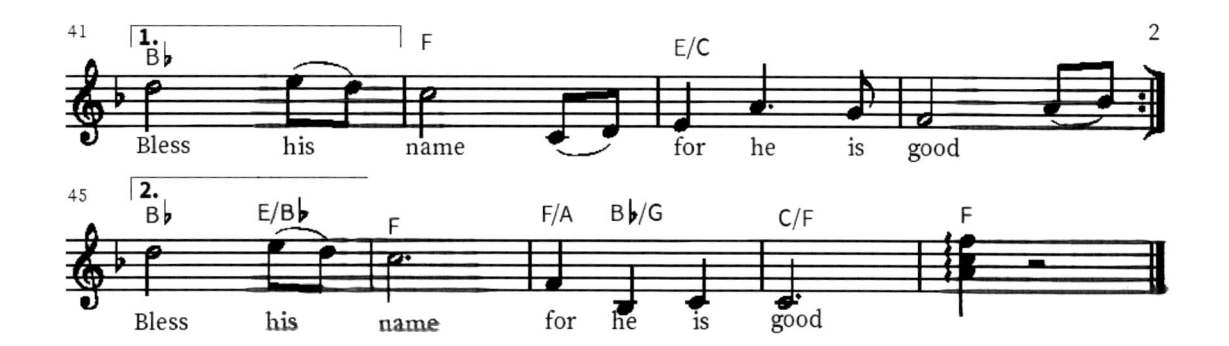

1. Bb | F | E/C |
Bless his name for he is good

45

2. Bb E/Bb | F | F/A Bb/G | C/F | F
Bless his name for he is good

Notes